D0776885

SEIZED by the SUN

Other Books in the Women of Action Series

SEIZED
by the SUN

THE LIFE AND DISAPPEARANCE OF
WORLD WAR II PILOT GERTRUDE TOMPKINS

★ ★ ★

James W. Ure

CHICAGO
REVIEW
PRESS

Published by Chicago Review Press Incorporated
814 North Franklin Street
Chicago, Illinois 60610
ISBN 978-1-61373-587-9

Library of Congress Cataloging-in-Publication Data

Names: Ure, James W., 1939– author.
Title: Seized by the sun : the life and disappearance of World War II pilot
    Gertrude Tompkins / James W. Ure.
Description: First edition. | Chicago, Illinois : Chicago Review Press
    Incorporated, 2017. | Series: Women of action | Includes bibliographical
    references and index.
Identifiers: LCCN 2016047279 (print) | LCCN 2016050005 (ebook) | ISBN
    9781613735879 (cloth) | ISBN 9781613735886 (adobe pdf) | ISBN
    9781613735909 (epub) | ISBN 9781613735893 (kindle)
Subjects: LCSH: Silver, Gertrude Tompkins, 1911–1944. | Women Airforce
    Service Pilots (U.S.)—Biography. | World War, 1939–1945—Participation,
    Female. | World War, 1939–1945—Aerial operations, American. | Air
    pilots, Military—United States—Biography. | Women air pilots—United
    States—Biography.
Classification: LCC D790.5 .U74 2017 (print) | LCC D790.5 (ebook) | DDC
    940.54/4973092 [B] —dc23
LC record available at https://lccn.loc.gov/2016047279

Interior design: Sarah Olson

Printed in the United States of America
5 4 3 2 1

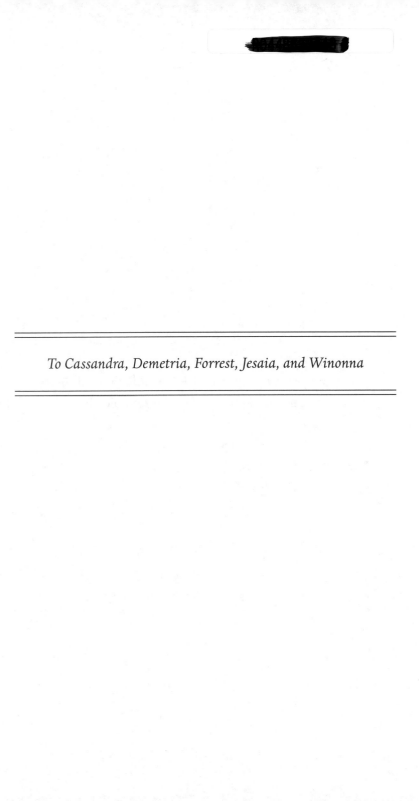

To Cassandra, Demetria, Forrest, Jesaia, and Winonna

The air up there in the clouds is very pure and fine, bracing and delicious. And why shouldn't it be? It is the same the angels breathe. —Mark Twain

CONTENTS

NOTE ON NAMES

Originally called the Air Service, today's US Air Force has undergone several name changes. It became the Air Corps in 1926, and the Air Corps became an element of the US Army Air Forces (USAAF) on June 20, 1941. USAAF continued to exist under command of the US Army until 1946—the time during which Gertrude Tompkins served. Readers will see frequent references to the army being in command of the air force.

The United States Air Force became an entity separate from the army on September 18, 1947. For the sake of simplicity, in this book "air force" will be used.

Women's Airforce Service Pilots are correctly abbreviated with the acronym WASP, in the singular. However, over time, books and stories written by WASP have added the *s* to the end of the word. It has become common usage to say and write WASPs, which is frequently used in this book.

Note that England and Britain are used interchangeably.

LOST WINGS

The new P-51D Mustang fighter plane rested on the Mines Field runway with its nose lifted to the sky. The shiny aluminum craft reflected the Southern California light, in spite of a haze that filtered the sun's rays.

A woman with gray eyes walked toward the aircraft. Her curly dark hair bounced lightly against the collar of her leather flight jacket. As a Women's Airforce Service Pilot, or WASP, Gertrude Tompkins's job was to fly this sleek plane across the country to Newark, New Jersey. From there it would be shipped to Europe for combat against Nazi Germany. It was brand new, one of 45 Mustangs that North American Aviation would have manufactured that day at its Los Angeles plant.

As a former test pilot, Gertrude, or Tommy, as her sister WASPs called her, knew how important her preflight inspection was. Even new planes had flaws. She slowly walked

1

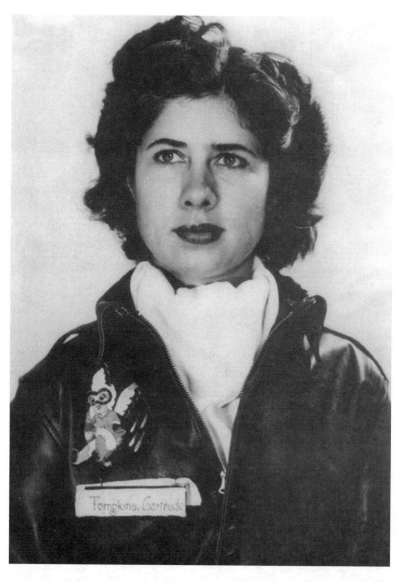

Gertrude "Tommy" Tompkins's official Women's Airforce Service
Pilots portrait. Note the Fifinella logo—the WASPs' cartoon mascot
designed by Walt Disney—on her leather flight jacket. *Courtesy of The
WASP Archives, Texas Women's University Libraries*

around the airplane. Gertrude pushed on the rudder to make certain it moved freely. Stooping, she tugged at a hydraulic line running through the scissor assembly over one of the 27-inch wheels. Every P-51 pilot made certain the line was tight. There had been reports of problems with Mustang wheels that wouldn't retract. She checked to be sure the tape was tight over the openings for the six .50-caliber Browning machine guns. The guns would be installed in Europe.

She walked around the left wing, touching the red running light, making certain the access compartment to the guns was tight and flush. It had a tendency to come off.

The woman gripped a hinged slot on the fuselage and lifted herself onto the wing. The cockpit yawned, waiting for her to settle in and fly away at 400 miles per hour.

Gertrude placed her small leather flight bag in the cockpit, working it alongside the seat amid the tight array of handles, toggles, tubes, and wires. The bag contained her PIF—Pilot's Information File. The PIF held weather information, maps, flight orders, and forms authorizing refueling and ground transportation. It also held first-aid supplies. As she tucked it away, Gertrude breathed in the new plane's smells: fresh paint and rubber, adhesives, and oil.

She knew how this plane would perform. The Mustang was a high-strung thoroughbred, a little balky at low speeds, but once free and running at full throttle, it would take your breath away. Gertrude climbed into the cockpit and settled in the metal bucket seat, using her parachute as her cushion. She latched the seat belt and shoulder harness.

Gertrude punched the ignition switch. The four-bladed propeller made a slow, hesitant turn. The exhaust ports exploded noisily, streaming acrid smoke back into the cockpit as the big paddles bit into the air faster and faster. She ran up the throttle. The engine reached a high-pitched snarl. The exhaust ports breathed clear now. It had come alive, this airplane, and was shivering to be away.

Next Gertrude set the altimeter, which would measure the plane's altitude. She flipped on the toggle switches for the radio and waited for its tubes to warm up. Squawks and static hisses filled her headset as she dialed in the sending and receiving frequency. She adjusted the silk scarf that pilots wore to prevent their necks from chafing against the collars of their leather flight jackets as they constantly swiveled their heads in flight.

A moment later, the control tower radioed her clearance for takeoff. Gertrude cranked the handle to bring the cockpit canopy forward. It snagged on something. She backed it off and tried again. After a couple of minutes she called the tower and told them she had a problem. Other WASPs were forming for takeoff in their P-51s; at least 30 of them would fly from Mines Field that day.

Factory-new airplanes often experienced problems. Most new planes were briefly tested after coming off the assembly line. Some were turned over to the WASP ferry pilots without any flight testing.

A Jeep screeched to a stop. Out leaped a North American Aviation factory technician. The mechanic examined the three tracks on which Gertrude's canopy rode and started making adjustments.

Since she was going to get a late start, Gertrude was redirected to the army air force base at Palm Springs, less than an hour's flight time in this swift craft. At Palm Springs she would "RON"—remain overnight—then continue to Newark tomorrow. Her mother and father lived in nearby Summit, New Jersey, and she planned to spend time with them after delivering the airplane.

Once airborne, she could consider her month-old marriage and her future. The familiar ring of the Mustang engine would soothe her. Flying gave her comfort and self-assurance. She was her own pilot, her own navigator, her own radio operator. Piercing the clouds on her race eastward, painful memories would fall away. Everything would be made right as she throttled up the 1,490-horsepower Rolls Royce Merlin engine. She wished the mechanic would hurry up and finish with the canopy.

IT'S AWFUL HAVING A STUTTER

Nothing in Gertrude Tompkins's early life or upbringing would hint that this well-bred girl would grow up to fly fighter planes. She came from a wealthy family with roots deep in New Jersey's Hudson River villages. The Vreeland farm was settled around the year 1658 by Gertrude's Dutch ancestors on her father's side. Gertrude's mother, Laura Towar, was born in 1878 into the well-off Bentley and Towar families of Jersey City Heights, both involved in finance in New York City. Laura's grandfather, Thomas Towar, who died in 1903, had a seat on the New York Stock Exchange, an expensive position purchased by a privileged few.

As a child Laura yearned for adventure, and she confessed that once she had wanted to become a missionary in China. "She was very strong minded in some ways, but was brought up in a repressive era," Laura's daughter Elizabeth Tompkins

Whittall recalled years later. "She had an easy life and was provided with servants all her life. Maybe she didn't feel useful. . . . Mother was nervous and had poor eyesight. She had to drop out of school. She had what she called nervous headaches." This undercurrent of depression and anxiety would continue to surface in Laura in the years to come.

Gertrude's father, Vreeland Tompkins, was a graduate of Rutgers University in New Brunswick, New Jersey. In 1894, at age 23, Vreeland was working for John D. Rockefeller's Standard Oil Company as a chemist. Because he stuttered badly, Vreeland was quiet and shy. He threw himself into his work. Each night he returned to his father's home at 533 Communipaw Avenue in Jersey City and in the basement puttered with chemical concoctions. Vreeland patented one of these mixtures. With a loan from his father he formed a company called Smooth-On to manufacture the compound, leaving Rockefeller's employment in 1895. Smooth-On Iron Cement was ideal for repairing leaks in cast iron and quickly became the industry standard for maintenance and repair. A contract with the US Navy for boiler repairs assured his fortune and the family's future. (Smooth-On Inc. is still in existence in Macungie, Pennsylvania, making molds and materials for a variety of applications, including special effects for motion pictures.)

It's uncertain how Vreeland Tompkins met the prettily freckled Laura Towar, but it is known that when he proposed to her in writing, she turned him down in writing. She felt she couldn't live with Vreeland's stuttering handicap. Later she changed her mind, and he agreed to leave his Dutch Reformed church to join her Episcopal church. They married on May 18, 1904, and purchased a three-story house at 113 Bentley Avenue in Jersey City. Its living room was big enough for their baby grand piano, which Laura loved to play. On the second floor were three bedrooms and two baths, one attached to the master bedroom.

Their first child, Stuart, died at birth, which tipped Laura into a lasting depression. "After she lost her first child, maybe it was just too much," her daughter Elizabeth later said. Life went on, and Margaret Tompkins arrived in 1906, blonde and bright-eyed. The witty Elizabeth was born in 1909. Gertrude, whose name in German means "strong spear," was born October 16, 1911. She was the last child born in the family.

From the beginning Gertrude had golden strands in her otherwise dark hair, a sure sign of her good fortune, her father said. To make certain the children were not spoiled, Vreeland and Laura maintained some distance from them. The parents were not demonstrative, leaving the care of the children to the servants. Vreeland and Laura routinely dined separately from their children.

By age four it was apparent that Gertrude was having difficulty with her speech. She had trouble getting her words out. Vreeland believed she must have inherited her stutter from him, and he felt both guilty and sorrowful.

Friends and family volunteered explanations for her stuttering. "It happened because you cut the child's hair before she said her first words," a relative insisted. "The child was frightened as a baby. Make her hold nutmeg under her tongue," suggested the family cook and nanny, Maggie. She and her husband, Thomas, who served as handyman, chauffeur, and gardener, occupied quarters on the third floor of the house.

Vreeland took a special interest in his youngest daughter. He had had difficulty being listened to when he was growing up. "S-s-someone else always said what I wanted to say

The Mystery of Stuttering

The definition of stuttering is to speak in such a way that the rhythm is interrupted by repetitions, blocks or spasms, or prolongations of sounds or syllables, sometimes accompanied by contortions of the face and body.

Specialists believe that stuttering can be managed through various therapies but that looking for a cure for stuttering is generally not realistic. A number of famous people are stutterers. The actress Emily Blunt and National Football League running back Darren Sproles manage their stuttering. Other stutterers include Marc Anthony, Nicole Kidman, and James Earl Jones. Winston Churchill and Marilyn Monroe were stutterers.

long before I could get it out," he complained. He insisted that everyone patiently wait as young Gertrude shyly spoke.

Her father vowed to get her the help that he had never gotten for his own speech difficulties and decided to send her to a doctor in Jersey City who claimed he could cure stuttering. The doctor put Gertrude through a brief speech exercise, slapping her cheek each time she stumbled over a word.

"If we do this every time she stutters, she'll eventually stop," the doctor said over the crying of the little girl. "I'll need to see her three times a week."

Her father fled in outrage, Gertrude in tow.

Another doctor in New York City examined Gertrude and said her tongue was too short. He offered three devices guaranteed to cure stuttering. The first was made of silver, inserted in the mouth, and worn around the neck. The second was a narrow, flattened tube of silver that fit across the roof of the mouth. Finally, there was a disk with a projecting silver tube that was placed between the lips. They were to be alternated until the cure was complete.

Vreeland considered these gadgets and may have tried them with Gertrude. Being a skeptical inventor and lifelong stutterer, he didn't have much faith in them.

The next specialist they visited was James Sonnet Greene, medical director of the National Hospital for Speech Disorders in New York. Greene believed that stuttering was not a speech disorder but a nervous disorder. To Vreeland, this sounded too much like her mother Laura's mental illness, and he would not have his daughter branded as mentally deficient. As a stutterer himself, he felt this diagnosis reflected on his own mental health, and he was not prepared to accept this notion.

Then they found Samuel Potter, a medical doctor and also a stutterer. Following his guidelines, Gertrude spent two to three hours daily on breathing exercises and vowel-consonant practice. Vreeland patiently helped his daughter and hired a special nurse to provide the required therapy. Nothing seemed to work.

Despite the challenges that came with Gertrude's stuttering, she also experienced some joyful times as a child. She became close to the household's two live-in servants, Maggie and Thomas. They came from Virginia, and they held

Gertrude and her sisters spellbound with their stories. Gertrude could sit for hours listening to Maggie's tales, and she watched with amusement as Thomas fell asleep in the middle of doing just about anything, including peeling potatoes. Her sister Elizabeth later wrote that the Tompkins girls never knew the last names of "this dear, sweet" couple.

Christmas brought excitement and joy that broke through the atmosphere of formality in the Tompkins household. After a breakfast the family trooped up the street to the home of the girls' grandmother Rosaline, Laura's mother. The living room door was closed, but through a crack they could see the glint of a bicycle or the wheel of a doll carriage. When the whole family was assembled according to age (youngest first), Laura played a march on the piano, and the children entered the room. Stockings were hung in a line across the marble fireplace. Only one gift was opened at a time. It was an hour of feverish excitement and fun for young Gertrude. After that, the family attended services at the Episcopal church.

Following a bountiful turkey dinner, they gathered in the parlor and played charades and word-guessing games. They also peered at Roman ruins through a stereopticon, a device that gave a three-dimensional appearance to specially printed photo cards. Christmas evening ended with a game of musical chairs, the family laughing and jostling for seats. On several Christmases, relatives of Thomas and Maggie joined them.

Gertrude became attuned to nuance, dialect, and lively expressions at a young age. Elizabeth noticed how Gertrude was able to repeat snatches of poems and songs without stuttering. Gertrude sang, "Things are seldom what they seem, skim milk masquerades as cream."

The family continued to search for stuttering cures. The book *Stuttering and Lisping* by Edward Wheeler Scripture had appeared in 1913. Using Scripture's guidelines, Gertrude was diagnosed by yet another doctor as having a type of stuttering caused by anxiety. Anxiety wasn't quite the same as Greene's "nervous disorder," and Vreeland could accept it because he knew from experience that stuttering and anxiety went hand in hand.

As part of Scripture's regimen, mild tonics of arsenic, quinine, and strychnine were given to little Gertrude. Many medicines of the day contained lethal as well as addictive ingredients. A nurse provided cold rubs, lukewarm or cold baths, sprays, moist packs, and massage. Gertrude was taken to Atlantic City for sea baths.

Despite some moments of joyful respite, the constant rounds of doctors and treatments during her youth made young Gertrude unhappy, everyone in the family agreed.

2

CHILDHOOD UPS AND DOWNS

Jersey City is home to the Bergen School for Girls, founded by Gertrude's grandmother Rosaline Bentley Towar and several of her civic-minded friends back in the 1870s. There was no question where Gertrude would be educated. The rambling school was a mile from her home. Six-year-old Gertrude walked there and back with her sisters every day. The classes were small, just eight girls in each, "so it was wise to do your homework every night," wrote her sister Elizabeth in her memoir, *From There to Here*.

Elizabeth described the active lives of the Tompkins children and recalled, "The mile walk to school, church, dancing school or music lessons etc. was normal. There were at least a dozen tennis courts in the nearby park and excellent ice skating on the lake there. . . . Between the edge of the park and the Jersey meadows was a wild strip which we explored each spring for wild flowers and migrating birds."

At first Gertrude found school pleasant, but her stutter soon changed that. When a teacher asked her to stand and read aloud, she flushed with anxiety and fear. She stuttered and stammered but successfully completed the page and sat down, among the titters of the other little girls.

Then she began to hear the other children chanting in the schoolyard at recess or on her way home:

>   *My n-n-n-name is Little Gertrude*
>   *And I-I-I-I am only three*
>   *Some p-p-p-people say I stutter*
>   *And n-n-n-no one cares for me*
>   *My m-m-m-m-mama used to stutter*
>   *When she m-m-m-married papa, too*
>   *It t-t-t-t took three days to marry,*
>   *'cause the p-p-p-p preacher stuttered too.*

She could never ask others to understand and help her. Her father's self-reliance and prideful ways were her ways, too. There was one bright spot: study of Latin and French began early at Bergen School, and Gertrude soon discovered that she seldom stuttered in foreign languages.

At home most mornings, the Tompkins girls were awakened by Maggie. After combing their hair and dressing, they trekked downstairs for a breakfast of hot cereal, supplemented by a tablespoon of sweet Maltine (a malt-based supplement) and cod liver oil, both considered guarantees of good health.

Each day after school, Gertrude and her sister Elizabeth walked hand in hand to Grandmother Rosaline's. The wealthy widow's imposing mansion sat on a hill that would later be called Jersey City Heights. The estate had stables, a large vegetable garden, extensive lawn and flower beds, and curved driveways with entrances on both Bentley and Harrison Avenues. Rosaline was a petite woman, but her voice came from deep within and her word was law. "Our whole family revolved around her," wrote Elizabeth.

Rosaline was said to be the last person in Jersey City to be driven by horse and carriage. Lady, the horse, clopped her way down Harrison Avenue, weaving between the honking autos as late as 1920. Grandmother Rosaline was old-fashioned

Entertainment, 1920s Style

Radio blasted into American homes in the 1920s. People listened to sports, comedy shows, and music. The first commercial radio station was Pittsburgh's KDKA, established in 1920. Three years later the country would have more than 500 commercial stations.

Movies were silent—accompanied by a piano or organ—until 1927. That year *The Jazz Singer* introduced synchronized sound. By the mid-1920s more than 50 million people would go to the movies each week—the equivalent of about half of America's population. Huge and elegant theaters were built all over America.

The phonograph also became popular in the 1920s, replacing the piano, a mainstay of family entertainment since the 1800s.

and rigid. When two cousins from New York came to pay their respects, Grandmother Rosaline refused to allow one of them inside because she had recently divorced. The divorced cousin was left outside to pace the porch.

Laura insisted that her daughters pay daily respects to their grandmother. They were told to ask how she was and what she was doing. If Grandmother Rosaline was in good spirits, the girls might be invited to stay. Sometimes she read to them from the Bible. On exceptional days, Rosaline allowed Patrick Fitzpatrick, her sometimes-sober gardener and chauffeur, to take them for a carriage ride.

Most days, Gertrude passed the time in the rooms of her own house. Thomas and Maggie and her sisters kept her busy as her mother lay in bed with severe headaches. Gertrude explored the dark, fragrant rooms of the cellar, where canned fruit and vegetables and coal were stored. Here was also a tiny bathroom used by the servants. Gertrude liked the fragrance of a tin of sweet-smelling powder that Maggie used to dust her underarms. Gertrude prowled the top floors, sneaking into Maggie and Thomas's bedroom, examining the little corn husk dolls the maid had collected.

As she grew older, a new sound filled the Tompkins's house. The family listened in rapt attention to voices and music that were broadcast from a radio in the living room. Gertrude learned to love classical music almost as much as she loved reading books.

Their mother's condition worsened as the girls grew older. The demands of a husband and three daughters weighed on her. One day when Gertrude was around 10, Laura refused to get out of bed. For the next two years she would remain ill in bed. Laura received treatment in a small, exclusive sanitarium in Cornwall, a community not far from West Point on New York's Hudson River. She stayed there frequently and sometimes for prolonged periods; other times she remained with the family.

While visiting Laura one weekend at the sanitarium, Vreeland found a farm for sale, a place in Mountainville, near Newburgh, New York. It was owned by Mr. Doxey, who had suddenly found himself bankrupt. Glenbrook Farm was 81 acres of woods, meadows, and apple orchards, with an old farmhouse, a perfect retreat for the family's summers. Vreeland bought the farm, and he built a small house for Doxey and his wife and paid them to stay and farm the land.

Preparing to move to the farm for the summer involved a joyous melee of family, animals, luggage, swimsuits, and hats. The girls and their English shepherd, Fritzy, climbed into Vreeland's Cadillac (he would have no other car) and drove the 50 miles to the farm on a warm May morning. There were cheers when Gertrude's father turned down the dirt road that followed a brook a quarter mile to the house.

Despite the shadow of their mother's illness, summers were carefree during the 10 years the family owned Glenbrook Farm. The three Tompkins girls explored, discovering three brooks, and Vreeland named one for each of them. On hot summer days the girls paddled and splashed in the creeks while their father visited Laura at the sanitarium. A tennis court was built at the farm, and the girls were able to tune up their games. Black currants grew abundantly and were fun to eat, their purple juices staining small hands and mouths. At the end of the day the girls were worn out from the sun and ready to be bathed by Marta, the Danish governess Vreeland hired to care for them during Laura's absence. As she toweled them off, the girls listened with fascination as Marta told them of dancing at Sunday evening balls in Copenhagen.

Two gardens at the farm produced tomatoes, carrots, radishes, and cucumbers, which Mr. Doxey frequently sent to the family when they were home in New Jersey. Each week he sent a shipment of fresh eggs, which arrived by Railway Express. They raised cows, pigs, and chickens and grew apples and berries. Just before Christmas each year Doxey killed the farm's hogs and sent some meat to the Tompkins family, including pigs' feet and pork jowl. Vreeland made the cook prepare all of it.

Elizabeth wrote of their time on the farm:

How blessed we were with all those acres to play in—woods, orchards, pastures, three brooks plus all the fascination of a working farm with cows, horses, pigs, chickens, an ice house, barns, a huge garden, a tennis court and swimming in Moodna Creek down the long winding driveway and across the main road. Yellow cream too thick to pour rose in large circular milk pans in the cool cellar off the kitchen. Making butter in the tall wooden churn was no chore at all. The skim milk was either put on the back of the stove to "clobber" or fed to the pigs. Early Sunday morning one of us was allowed to make the ice cream. It was a simple mixture of cream and crushed berries or other fruit from the farm packed in rock salt. Turning the handle a few times was all there was to it. My, how rich and good it tasted.

Gertrude's school months were not nearly as carefree as her summers. An average pupil, her days at school were lonely, in spite of the efforts of Miss Van Cleef and Miss Moira, the headmistresses of the school, who exhibited a genuine affection for the girl with the gray eyes. At home she wanted so much to hug her father. She loved him. He did so much for her. She worked at pleasing him, but he remained archly formal and always just out of reach.

Gertrude's mother found short periods of calmness and escaped her inner demons when home by working in the garden, enjoying the heady fragrance of the loamy soil and digging her fingers deep into the earth. Each fall she planted the daffodils and tulips that bordered the garden, and she loved dropping each bulb into carefully sculpted cups in the soil. Gertrude helped with the planting.

The search for a cure for Gertrude's stutter continued. Yet another doctor prescribed a new regimen. For one week Gertrude was made to keep silent. The second week she was allowed to whisper, louder and louder, until at last she could speak at full volume. It did nothing to cure or even help her stuttering.

As Gertrude entered third grade her father tried yet another cure. Vreeland had come across another book on stuttering, this one called *Home Cure for Stammerers* by George Lewis. As a result, Gertrude's regimen now included rising at 6:30 AM and drinking a glass of water while dressing. Then she was taken on a brisk walk in the open air, even when the temperatures were below freezing. Breakfast followed but with no coffee or tea allowed. The diet provided only stale bread for breakfast, and it had to be consumed slowly, under her father's watchful eye. She missed the hot, milky cereal that Maggie fixed for her.

At noon she was supervised as she sipped one glass of water slowly. At dinner she had to avoid fatty substances and unripe food. Afterward, at Vreeland's request, she read aloud to the family from *Huckleberry Finn*: "We catched fish and talked, and we took a swim now and then to keep off sleepiness. It was kind of solemn, drifting down the big, still river, laying on our backs and looking up at the stars."

After a year with no apparent results, Vreeland consulted another doctor. Now Gertrude was made to read aloud through clenched teeth, five minutes each day at first, adding five more minutes until she reached 60 minutes total. Vreeland and Laura both thought it helped, and he encouraged Gertrude to keep at it. She followed this therapy for years. She kept it up to please her father, the man she was certain loved her. Her stuttering continued unabated, but she lost herself in the works she read aloud: Shakespeare, Ralph Waldo Emerson, Walter Scott, and the poetry of William Wordsworth and William Blake. By age 13 Gertrude could often be found curled in an overstuffed chair in the parlor reading, as the sleet of an Atlantic storm buffeted the big house.

In 1926 Grandmother Rosaline died, succumbing to diabetes. Fifteen-year-old Gertrude watched with morbid interest as her sister Elizabeth, who was said to have a "way" with hair, styled the snow-white tresses of the corpse. At the funeral, the priest whispered to Vreeland that he'd heard that Gertrude's stutter might have been caused by making her switch from being left-handed to right-handed. This puzzled Vreeland, for Gertrude had always been right-handed. The priest said that if she were made to hold a penny under her tongue, it might cure her.

Rosaline's death seemed to liberate Laura Tompkins. The long, assertive shadow of her mother was gone. Laura grew stronger daily, and she no longer remained confined to bed. In opposition to what her mother would have wished, she joined the American Birth Control League (ABCL)—an organization founded by activist Margaret Sanger in 1921 and devoted to encouraging women to take control of their own fertility and reproduction—and even founded a clinic in Newark. Eventually the ABCL would become Planned Parenthood, and Laura remained active in that organization until her death at 93.

When it came to the sex education of her own daughters, however, Laura had difficulty talking to them. "When I reached the appropriate age she handed me a book [about sex] and that was that," wrote Elizabeth. Gertrude received a copy of the same book.

As a teenager Gertrude's stuttering only grew worse. Sometimes she couldn't speak for several seconds. As she waited for the words to come, others tried to encourage the words from her lips, saying, for example, "Do you mean 'hotel'? Or are you trying to say 'home'?" She felt shamed by her inability to speak as others did. She shrank from people and avoided speaking in class. Eventually, her teachers no longer called on her. Often Gertrude said she was ill and stayed home from school.

Vreeland found consolation in the fact that his daughter's stutter was less severe than his own. He cheerfully deluded himself that he could see some improvement and results were soon to come. In fact, his daughter simply resisted speaking. But as she reached young adulthood, the seeds of confidence would be planted in an unexpected place.

3

CONFIDENCE GROWS

Spring brought a flush of emerald to the hardwoods in Jersey City. Gertrude often read in the afternoon sun as her mother worked in her flower beds.

"Give her enough books, she'll educate herself," Headmistress Van Cleef told Vreeland.

But in spite of her reading, Gertrude's grades were sinking.

The family was preparing to move from the home in congested Jersey City to the community of Summit, a suburb to the west. Gertrude feared entering a new school where she would be subjected to new humiliation as her classmates discovered her stutter.

To make matters worse, she was being deserted by her sister and closest friend, Elizabeth, who was going away to Wellesley College, located west of Boston. (Margaret was already in her third year at Smith College in Massachusetts).

Gertrude had become comfortable with the patterns of family living in the big house.

The move was completed in 1927. The house at 174 Summit Avenue was more imposing than the old place in Jersey City. Gertrude fell deeper into a depression, and her father worried that she might have inherited Laura's condition.

Often Gertrude said she felt ill, and she spent the day in her bed reading. When she did trudge to school, she dragged home at the end of the day and buried herself in her novels and poetry. It was a gloomy existence, and the only lift she got was from her books. During her junior year of high school she was often absent, and she did only what she had to do to pass her courses. Her teachers pressed Vreeland to challenge the girl. Her senior year was the same. She refused to speak in class and read her novels instead of her texts. One teacher said she should be expelled, and for a few weeks this threat seemed to rouse her to do better work, while making her feel worse than ever.

When boys tried to talk to Gertrude, she turned them away with a shake of her head.

At age 18 her stutter was as bad as it ever was. She never wanted to visit another specialist again. Vreeland, persistently pursuing every avenue of relief, took Gertrude to a psychiatrist in New York City, Dr. Margaret Kenworthy. The psychiatrist refused to allow the parents in the room during her sessions with their daughter. The doctor asked who Gertrude liked best in the family, and then who was next, and so on down the line of siblings.

"It was a disaster. Instead of helping, it turned the family upside down. Gertrude became defiant and independent. She threatened to quit school," said Elizabeth.

Dr. Kenworthy told Vreeland that Gertrude needed to be away from the pressures of her family and recommended she spend time on a farm in the country. Vreeland had sold Glenbrook Farm, so he sent his daughter instead to be with a family on a farm in the beautiful Shenandoah Valley region of western Virginia, but he never took Gertrude to Dr. Kenworthy again.

In the spring of 1930, when Gertrude arrived at the farm, flowering trillium plants would have covered the hardwood slopes of Virginia's mountain ridges, lending a frothy look to the famous indigo hue of the hills. The oak and hickory forest and mountain laurel would have formed tunnels over the twisting roads, and pink rhododendrons would have glowed like spirits in the thickets.

At the farm, Gertrude made a friend of one of the local girls, according to Elizabeth. Together, they may have explored the Shenandoah's hollows and hillsides and spotted or heard stories about native plants such as chicory, yarrow, and butterfly weed said to have healing properties. The locals must have warned her about wild boar, bobcats, copperheads, and timber rattlers.

Gertrude's stay on the Virginia farm coincided with the start of the Great Depression in America. During the Depression rural poverty touched everyone. A farm's chickens and cows provided an important part of the family diet. Dresses were made of feed bags. Many people went shoeless. City residents drove to the country to barter used clothing for fruits and vegetables grown by the farmers. There was one important cash crop in Virginia: distilleries hidden in the backwoods supplied an abundance of whiskey. Drinking alcohol was illegal in America from 1919 to 1933. During Prohibition drinkers turned to rural bootleggers for illegal alcohol, called moonshine.

Gertrude's family welcomed the peace that came with her exile. They hoped that their troubled girl from the industrial thickets of New Jersey might begin to find herself in the mountains of Virginia. Her sister said that while Gertrude claimed to have hated her year in Virginia, it clearly stimulated her interest in farming and gardening. Nature seemed to focus her. Sometime during her year there, she filled out an application for admission to the Pennsylvania School of Horticulture for Women. It was located in Ambler, just north of Philadelphia. A small school, it seemed safe and personal. In spite of her mediocre high school grades, Gertrude was accepted at Ambler.

Vreeland, whose other daughters were at the prestigious colleges Smith and Wellesley, exclaimed, "And *you* want to be a farmer?" Her mother intervened on Gertrude's behalf, saying, "It's the first thing she's taken a serious interest in, and she should be allowed to enroll in the school." Vreeland relented and supported his daughter at Ambler.

Gertrude arrived on the Ambler campus dressed in a suit, hat, and gloves. Her mother and father accompanied her, and the Cadillac carried her suitcases and a steamer trunk, a large wooden box with a rounded top that was banded with leather or more wood to make it sturdy.

The Pennsylvania School of Horticulture for Women was founded in 1910 by June Bowne Haines, a graduate of Bryn Mawr College, which is also located near Philadelphia. Bowne Haines had visited several English gardening schools earlier in the 20th century and determined that horticulture should be part of American education. She acquired an initial 71 acres with the financial support of friends. The school flourished, attracting students from Germany, Australia, and even Japan. In 1929 the school built its first campus dormitory.

The year 1930 was not the most auspicious time for Gertrude to arrive at college. The Great Depression was spreading economic misery. Though many causes contributed to the Depression, the stock market crash in 1929 was the lynchpin of a calamity that was felt around the world. The unemployment rate soon reached 25 percent of all Americans. Men lost their jobs and couldn't buy food. Banks failed. For women workers conditions were terrible. In Chicago, women workers were paid less than 25 cents an hour, and one-fourth of them received less than 10 cents an hour. In some states tax revenue was so low that school was conducted only three days a week. The British economist John Maynard Keynes was asked if there had ever been anything like the Depression before. "Yes," he said, "it was called the Dark Ages and it lasted 400 years."

On arriving at Ambler, Gertrude and her fellow students were restricted from taking baths due to the drought, which was "terrible all over," as Gertrude wrote to her sister Elizabeth in a lengthy letter dated October 26, 1930.

Elizabeth was having an adventure of her own, teaching at the American School for Girls in Damascus, Syria. While visiting friends in Lebanon, she had met Guy Whittall, a manager for Royal Dutch Shell. They were married on November 18, 1930.

Gertrude wrote Elizabeth about how they unexpectedly received relief from the drought in the form of rain that lasted all night, and the girls gathered in the recreation hall. One of them composed a "hymn to mother rain." Soon the girls were heartily singing, and Gertrude joined, never fearing her stutter when in song. There was a comic quality to this moment of bonding, and in the letter to Elizabeth she conveyed a newfound if tentative happiness. Her fellow students were friendly, and if any of them made fun of her stuttering she made no mention of it.

Gertrude described her studies: "We must learn at least three Latin names for every vegetable, tree, flower and bug. The bugs are the worst: [I] hate the things anyway and to hunt for them is awful." She was introduced to double digging, a system whereby the gardener digs two spade lengths into the soil to turn it.

On the weekend, she related, she went to a movie in Ambler and saw *All Quiet on the Western Front*, a film about a German soldier's experiences during World War I. "It was ghastly in some parts, but not as bad as the book."

She found other Ambler students who shared her love of tennis, but the school's clay court was lumpy and needed compressing. She expressed her regret to Elizabeth that she would never "catch up to you at the rate my tennis is progressing." She also asked, "Have you ridden a camel or an Arabian horse yet?" and "Have you had any real Syrian food?"

Unseasonably cold weather came with the rains, which meant Gertrude was stuck in her dorm room or the recreation area much of the time. "I am making mittens violently and knit all the time when I ought to be doing something else." She drank tea with her closest friend at Ambler, Mia Ely, and together they listened to the popular New York Philharmonic Symphony on the radio every Sunday afternoon, "Just like we were at home."

She mentioned other friends. "Peggy Bean is the nicest girl in school. She is a senior. She is the kind of person who is darling to everybody and it comes perfectly naturally. By the way, she is my hair dresser and washes my hair almost as well as you do. We have lots of fun doing it in the tubs in the basement and using a watering can to rinse it." A Chinese student, Chi Chow, prepared chow mein for the girls, but it made them all ill.

Gertrude wrote about her introduction to animal husbandry. The school kept a herd of about 10 cows, and the young women watched the birth of a Jersey bull calf, "the sweetest little bull there ever was. Nearly all the cows are expecting a calf sometime in the near future, which is a very exciting prospect."

She described a slice of her life at Ambler:

I made a compost pile. The latter is quite an art. It must be absolutely square and about four feet high. It was made from a heap of rotten vegetables, chicken manure, dead mice and . . . everything imaginable all put between layers of decaying straw. It must be stamped down once in a while to get it packed solid. . . . Then in floriculture we transplanted peonies. Slews and slews of them, and you know how deep peony roots go. . . . We have been making cider quite a bit lately. It is lots of fun but awfully hard work turning the press, but I am glad it is because I'd like to have really strong arms.

If you find any lotion or anything like that in Damascus to make hands beautiful please let me know as mine are perfect sights. My fingers are all getting full of little black lines. The only saving grace is doing lots of laundry but we aren't supposed to wash anything now on account of the drought.

At the beginning of Gertrude's second year, a number of her friends did not return to Ambler. The Depression had the country in its grip, and many students could no longer afford to attend. However, there were still wealthy people in America who were untouched by the Depression. Barbara Hutton, heiress to the Woolworth dime store fortune, had a coming-out party at the Ritz Hotel in New York City in 1933 that cost $1 million in today's currency. Famous singer Rudy Vallee provided vocals, and the guests danced to four orchestras. Eucalyptus and silver birch trees were imported from California for the evening. A list of the rich and famous

The Depression and Music

The music business came close to collapsing during the Depression. In Chicago, shivering, jobless men burned old phonograph records to keep warm. American record companies, which had sold more than 100 million copies a year in the mid-1920s, were selling just 6 million by 1933.

Swing—a type of jazz but with a new name—became popular. Dances included the big apple and little peach, the shag and Susy Q, and the dance that had started it all—the Lindy hop. They would all become known as jitterbugging.

The melancholy sounds of "Happy Days Are Here Again" and Kate Smith singing "God Bless America" expressed hope for better times.

in attendance included the Astors and the Rockefellers, both families of great wealth.

Vreeland's Smooth-On business was not yet feeling the economic pinch. Early in the Depression it was frequently cheaper to maintain older cast-iron equipment than to purchase it new. However, cast iron was giving way to steel, aluminum, and other new metals and alloys. Even in decline, Smooth-On did well enough that Vreeland was able to continue to provide the family with a comfortable living and pay for Gertrude's schooling. She graduated from the Pennsylvania School of Horticulture for Women and was named in school records as one of the founders of the Woman's National Farm and Garden Association, New Jersey Division.

After Ambler, Gertrude made a brief visit back to Virginia. Perhaps she saw the terrible effects of the Depression in the rural communities there: skinny children, tattered clothes, cars parked where they ran out of gas and now providing nests for chickens and spiders. Men hunted out of necessity, and if they got a squirrel, the family ate stew. If not, they ate boiled dandelion greens. As she drove along the Shenandoah in the Chevrolet her parents had given her, she must have passed dozens of abandoned farms.

Politically, Gertrude found herself in conflict with her father, who was a vocal critic of President Franklin D. Roosevelt and his New Deal. In spite of President Herbert Hoover calling him "a madman," Roosevelt was elected in a landslide over Hoover in 1932. For Gertrude, Roosevelt seemed the only hope for millions. She and Elizabeth both shared Roosevelt's view that every American should have four freedoms: freedom of speech, freedom of worship, freedom from want, and freedom from fear. Vreeland, a captain of industry,

Franklin D. Roosevelt

Franklin D. Roosevelt, a man immobilized by polio in 1921, thundered into action when he became president in 1933. His first 100 days were a whirlwind of activity. He gave 10 major speeches and created a dozen new agencies designed to fight the Depression. He herded through Congress 13 major pieces of legislation, including insurance for all bank deposits, refinancing of home mortgages, Wall Street reforms, and authorization for nearly $4 billion in federal relief. He ended Prohibition and legalized the public sale of alcohol. He passed laws creating the Civilian Conservation Corps (CCC), the Agricultural Adjustment Administration (AAA), and the Tennessee Valley Authority (TVA).

"Take a method and try it," he said. He was improvising. Some of his actions would help, some would be found unconstitutional, and some would be ineffective. He would be reelected four times and would see America through the most difficult part of the 20th century.

a board member of Rutgers University, and a conservative Republican, felt unsettled by his daughter's progressive views and wondered if the Communists had influenced the Pennsylvania horticultural school. "One Roosevelt was one too many," he grumbled, referring to an earlier Roosevelt president, Franklin's distant cousin Theodore.

Gertrude was inspired by Roosevelt. His handicap hadn't stopped him. Why should hers? She became more confident and assertive, and she was moved to seek new adventures.

4

TRAVELING ABROAD

For young women of wealth, it was common to travel after graduating from college. Gertrude's family encouraged her to see Europe, and she finally agreed with a vague plan of visiting the sites where her ancestors had lived in England and Holland. Like most young American women from wealthy families, she was accompanied by a traveling companion: her aunt.

Once aboard a steamship, Gertrude became captivated by the idea of her passage through time and across the sea without having to meet the expectations of others. The water hissing beneath the hull of the ship soothed her, and the moon reflecting off the Atlantic felt romantic. Gertrude doubted she would ever marry. Her speech impediment would see to that. She agreed with Vreeland that perhaps her speech problems were inherited, and she thought it would not be a good thing

Traveling Companions

Traveling companions, also known as a lady's companion, existed until as late as the mid-20th century. A companion was usually someone from the same upper social strata as the woman she was paid to accompany. She was expected to make conversation and be sociable. She was not a servant but rather served as a chaperone and was assumed to be someone who could intervene in case of unwanted male attention.

For example, in the 1908 novel *A Room with a View* by E. M. Forster, Miss Bartlett was Lucy Honeychurch's cousin and was enlisted to accompany her on a trip abroad.

to bring another stuttering child into the world. Besides, she felt undesirable, and she avoided the young men who tried to approach her on the ship. She would keep on traveling, keep ahead of the pain that human beings brought into her life. She liked creatures, plants, and trees better than humans, anyway.

In London she found herself part of a group of tourists from the ship that clung together like a herd of sheep, hurrying from cathedral to cathedral. After visiting Kensington Gardens on a cold and gloomy day, she felt depressed and restricted by the group. The garden visit had given her an idea, stimulating her courage to see things she had read about at Ambler.

Early the next day she and her aunt quietly slipped away from their hotel. By midday they had crossed the English Channel on a boat. They took a train from Calais to Paris, where Gertrude immediately fell in love with the elegant gardens that graced the City of Light. She strolled in the Garden of the Royal Palace. She was enchanted by the tiny Square du Vert-Galant near Notre-Dame. She spent her days marveling at the gardens of the Tuileries and Versailles, as well as the Luxembourg Gardens. "She fell in love with all of it," said her sister Elizabeth.

One of her subjects at Ambler had been Renaissance gardens, and her fascination with them led her south to Italy. The gardens of Italy enchanted her. She sketched for hours, admiring the symmetry, the clever designs in stone and greenery, the subtle glow of opening flowers, the cascading water, the precise stonework that harmonized with the water features. She took notes, moving each day to a different garden, feeling rich with new knowledge and experience.

Sometimes a garden's owners would see the young American scratching away in her notebook, and frequently she was asked to have tea or dine with them. Often the locals provided a history of the gardens that she would never have gotten from her textbooks. She gained a new confidence and rapidly picked up Italian—stutter-free. That was another benefit of travel: she never stuttered in a foreign language. In Rome she visited the Vatican Gardens, the decaying estates of Maxentius's country house on the Appian Way, and the expansive Villa Borghese gardens.

The Roman Forum stunned her with its ancientness. She liked these ruined gardens best, the ancient remnants of pillars—some tumbled, some broken—on which sprouted

grasses and shrubs. She sat beneath a wisteria, marveling at
its huge and ancient trunk, the way its purple and pink blos-
soms entwined the columns of the Temple of Castor and Pol-
lux. Perhaps she heard the echo of the ancient Roman voices.
She may have felt sad for Emperor Claudius, also a stutterer,
as she gazed on the crumbling House of Livia, dedicated to
his cunning and probably murderous stepmother.

She marveled at the scarlet profusion of poppies rising
along the Italian railroad tracks and sent a sketch of the poppies to her sister. She stayed a few days in Venice, her artist's
eye no doubt admiring the lemon-hued sky created by the
lagoon's reflection. Later, Gertrude trekked along the Amalfi
Coast to admire the terraced farms of olive and orange trees.
She loved the Italian people but was critical of their leader,
Benito Mussolini. During the time Gertrude was in Italy,
Mussolini was conducting aerial bombing on Ethiopia.

She was intoxicated with the heady mix of nature and history, and she was determined to continue her journeys. She
lived in the moment while traveling, and the past and the
future did not seem to exist.

For the next several years Gertrude was on the move,
crisscrossing the Atlantic on ships. She loved the fjords of
Norway. In Copenhagen she watched the streets turn to riv-
ers of people riding bicycles. In the Netherlands she visited
Haarlem, where Vreeland's ancestors had lived before leaving for America. She toured Germany. She took a boat up the
Rhine and marveled at the ancient castles and the estates.

She returned to France and visited vineyards. On impulse
one sunny fall afternoon, she left her guide and joined
grape pickers in the vineyard. She spent the afternoon with

the workers, laughing and picking grapes, sharing jokes in French, which sometimes had to be explained to her.

Am I avoiding the person who I must become? Gertrude frequently asked herself this question, according to Elizabeth. By traveling she could stay ahead of her self-doubt and set aside her anxiety about the future.

Somewhere in Switzerland she met a woman goatherd who introduced her to a breed of goat called Saanen, named after the Saanen Valley in that country. Gertrude was so fascinated by this breed that she became determined to raise goats when she returned to the United States.

5

FINDING HER FOOTING

True to her dream, Gertrude bought two Saanen goats and established them at the family home in Summit, to the dismay of her father. Raising goats in urban New Jersey proved difficult. Two goats produced only a few quarts of milk a day, hardly enough to distribute to stores. Priced at 80 cents a quart, income never exceeded expenses, as Vreeland pointed out to his daughter, especially since she insisted on giving so much of the milk away.

Gertrude had placed a classified newspaper ad offering goat's milk. There were some regular purchasers. A man, woman, and baby appeared at the door, asking to buy the milk. They had taken a bus to get to Summit from their home in Jersey City. Their baby was allergic to cow's milk. Gertrude cut the price of her milk by half, and the couple

Why Gertrude Loved Goats

Goats can indeed make good pets—if you have space for them. Some can even be housebroken. They need shelter outdoors from the weather and like clean water and fresh grass and leaves. Goats seem to enjoy hiking with their owners. They will even carry a pack for your picnic lunch. They can be led on a leash, are very sure-footed, are notorious for undoing simple gate closures, will respond to their names, and may live up to 30 years. A young female goat is called a doeling, and a young male is called a buckling. Any goat under six months is called a kid.

returned frequently. Her father accused her of being too soft-hearted to be a proper businesswoman.

The neighbors complained. It seemed the goats were great climbers and had gotten over fences and into the neighbors' flower and vegetable gardens. City officials sent an inspector to the house, and Gertrude was warned about keeping goats. She responded to the city council that many townspeople kept chickens and that there were even a few cows tended by families in Summit. But goats were too much for the city leaders.

She found a goat breeder in Morris Plains who agreed to take her goats, which she visited regularly. She remained an enthusiastic advocate, and she took the health benefits of goat's milk the public.

Elizabeth and her husband, Guy Whittall, had by now moved from his company posting in Madagascar to Cape Town, South Africa. Gertrude arrived for a visit in 1933. Elizabeth's daughter Penny was an infant, and 22-year-old Gertrude was beguiled by the baby and assisted a nurse in caring for her.

Spending two months in South Africa, Gertrude spoke to women's groups. Over tea she stuttered out her enthusiasm for the benefits of goat milk, especially for infants. She found that she thought less about her stutter since she had become involved in promoting the health benefits of goat's milk to the public. She had become less self-conscious about it, said Elizabeth. Gertrude was feeling a new sense of confidence.

Leaving Cape Town, Gertrude traveled up Africa's eastern coast to visit the game parks in Kenya, and then went on to Turkey. She spent six weeks visiting Guy Whittall's family in Izmir, then called Smyrna. After that, her travels took her to New Zealand, where she made a hit with the press. An undated New Zealand newspaper article about her read in part:

GOATS AS A HOBBY
AMERICAN VISITOR'S CHOICE
ONCE LANDSCAPE GARDNER

Keeping goats as a profitable hobby in preference to following her original avocation of landscape gardening, for which she holds a diploma, is the unusual choice for Miss Gertrude Tompkins, a young American visitor from New York, who arrived in Auckland by the Monterey, states our Sydney correspondent. Miss Tompkins is a wealthy American girl who, when she is not attending to her goat farm in New Jersey, spends most of her time travelling abroad. Goats' milk is increasing in demand in the United States . . . and is a sound economic proposition. . . .

Miss Tompkins, who was accompanied by her aunt, Miss Towar of New York, spent several weeks motoring through New Zealand. . . . One of her most pleasant recollections is of a visit to the model pa [village] of Princess Te Puea Herangi at Ngaruawahia. Since then she has been a devoted exponent of the poi.

"I consider poi dancing to be one of the most graceful forms of recreation for girls that I have seen in any part of the world," she declared. . . . As a memento of her visit to Ngaruawahia, Miss Tompkins carried away with her a beautiful piece of greenstone, a gift from the Maori princess.

In 1936 polio struck Elizabeth Tompkins Whittall, then living in Cairo. Elizabeth sailed back to the United States in September, and Gertrude became her companion throughout the next year, providing mostly company and moral support since Elizabeth had a nurse to care for her physically. Elizabeth would always carry the effects of polio in her right leg, but she never lost her sense of adventure or her interesting lifestyle. She and her husband were next posted to Bermuda by Royal Dutch Shell. While there they entertained famous people, including the photographer Yousuf Karsh, the flier Jimmy Doolittle, and playwright Noël Coward. She did volunteer work for the National Association for the Advancement of Colored People (NAACP) and later, like her mother, for Planned Parenthood.

Gertrude Tompkins in
about 1938. *Courtesy of
the Whittall family*

When not traveling,
Gertrude lived in Sum-
mit with her parents. She
still considered goats her
passion, but Smooth-On,
her father's company, was
now experiencing diffi-
cult times. The Depression had finally caught up with Iron
Cement. Vreeland could no longer support her travels.

To help her father, and to "keep the money in the family,"
as Vreeland put it, Gertrude offered to work for Smooth-On.
She was 28 years old, and it was time to move out of the family home. The independence fostered by her travel caused her
to feel closed in when she was in her parents' home, and with
her work at Smooth-On she was able to support herself for
the first time. She decided to live in New York City and commute to the Smooth-On offices in Jersey City.

Gertrude went apartment hunting. She found a place she
liked in Greenwich Village, a double brownstone at historic
94 MacDougal Street, the MacDougal-Sullivan Gardens. Each
building had a small courtyard, and there was a common garden for all of the brownstones. The owner of her building, a
Yale graduate named Henry M. Silver, introduced himself. In
addition to being her landlord, he was an editor at Columbia

University Press. Friendly and smart, he and Gertrude shared a love of history and gardening.

From her apartment Gertrude's commute to Smooth-On took about 30 minutes. She paid a nickel to ride the subway under the Hudson River to Jersey City. At Smooth-On she managed company correspondence, handled government paperwork, and prepared sales letters.

She took delight in furnishing her new apartment by searching secondhand stores. Her mother insisted that her sofa and bed be new, so she bought them on the installment plan and felt very modern. At night she returned to her apartment on MacDougal and listened to symphonies on the radio while she read.

Greenwich Village was a hotbed of unrest in the late 1930s. The Communists had their American headquarters there. So did the Socialist Workers Party. The American Student Union, a group of independent, left-wing students who opposed militarism, operated in the Village. Poets and musicians haunted the smoky jazz clubs. One can imagine how Gertrude's conservative father must have viewed this environment.

Since Gertrude had to pass Henry Silver's apartment every day, he often popped out to greet her, making small talk and dropping puns, which he loved ("Deceit is a place to sit down. Defense is what keeps de dog in"). He wanted to take her out for a drink. She said no. He asked her to go to a movie. She declined.

Henry Silver was 10 years older than Gertrude, and he was recently divorced. His manner was engaging, but she was not interested in a romance with him. He explained how he once stuttered too and told her of his childhood speech problem, which he eventually outgrew. Henry, she learned, had been raised in Manhattan. His father, whom Henry called "Sir," was a doctor. He'd grown up in a Victorian home, with stringent social repressions. Like Gertrude, Henry knew his father would be appalled if he knew of Henry's support for FDR and the New Deal.

Henry wooed her ardently, but Gertrude simply felt no love for him, and the thought of marriage frightened her. Marriage in 1939 usually meant becoming a housewife and not having your own money. It meant giving up travel on one's own. Gone would be Gertrude's goats, which she still visited on weekends. Marriage meant subordinating herself to a man, just as her mother had done.

Conscious of Gertrude's passion for classical music, Henry used it to his advantage. He proposed an evening at the symphony to Vreeland and Laura. They accepted. How could Gertrude say no after her parents had consented? Thus she was roped into her first date with Henry through the unknowing involvement of her parents.

Henry had an insatiable intellectual curiosity, and it extended to Vreeland's business. He asked many questions about Smooth-On. Vreeland and Laura liked Henry from the start, but Gertrude's heart was about to be captured by someone—and something—else entirely.

6

TAKING FLIGHT

Reading the pages of the *New York Times* in 1939 and 1940, Gertrude saw hints of cultural changes coming to America. A young singer named Frank Sinatra made his debut. Animated motion pictures were a hit, with Walt Disney's full-length *Pinocchio* premiering in New York City, to be followed later that year by *Fantasia*. McDonald's opened its first restaurant in San Bernardino, California. Bugs Bunny made his first appearance in "Wild Hare."

While America was struggling to pull itself out of the Great Depression, war was about to ravage Europe, where trouble had been simmering for years. Gertrude could not have known that the conflicts brewing across the Atlantic Ocean would soon change the course of her life.

In Germany, Adolf Hitler rose to power through political intimidation and brutality. Many who openly opposed the policies of his Nazi Party were beaten or imprisoned; some were murdered. Becoming chancellor in 1934, Hitler claimed to represent a new Germany, one rising from the ashes of the 1918 German defeat in World War I. Hitler stabilized the German dollar, called the deutsche mark. (At one time the deutsche mark had become so inflated that it took a wheelbarrow load of bills to buy a loaf of bread.) He ordered the construction of superhighways, called autobahns. The economy became more robust as unemployed Germans found jobs. Factories began gearing up for a new war.

One of history's most infamous dictators, Hitler was born in Austria in 1898. While serving a prison term for political agitation in 1923, he wrote a book called *Mein Kampf,* which translated means "my struggle." In it he blamed Jewish people for most of Europe's ills and spelled out his vision for a new Germany.

France and England had been weakened by the Great Depression and had no stomach for another war. Between them they had 8 million people killed or wounded in World War I. They expressed their concerns over Hitler's aims but remained passive in the face of the dictator's broken promises.

Hitler flouted the terms that the Treaty of Versailles imposed on Germany at the end of World War I, which was often called "the war to end all wars." He defiantly took over areas of northern France and Czechoslovakia. Austria was absorbed into Germany and ceased to exist as a country.

Hitler also made a pact with Soviet Russia, which was led by the dictator Joseph Stalin. Together Soviet Russia and Germany invaded Poland in September 1939. England and France reluctantly came to Poland's aid. World War II had been ignited and would rage for the next six years.

Germany quickly conquered Poland, Denmark, Norway, Holland, Belgium, and France. England refused to surrender and retreated to its home islands to rebuild its military.

Germany signed war treaties with Japan and Italy, forming what was called the Axis. They vowed to support one another. By 1940 the Axis seemed invincible.

Russia remained independent but had gained much eastern European land from its alliance with Germany.

Japan's government was under the control of a militant faction. This small island nation needed coal, oil, and metals that they could only get from other countries. They took these countries by force. Beginning in 1931 they occupied large areas of China. Japan also occupied islands in the western Pacific called the Mariana Islands.

In the summer of 1941 Germany surprised the world and invaded Russia, its former ally, rolling up victory after victory against Stalin's troops. By autumn of 1941 it appeared that only England and the United States stood between the Axis and their conquest of the world. But America was reluctant to enter the fray.

In the 1930s a majority of Americans thought the United States should avoid another European war. Over 320,000 American troops had been killed or wounded in France in World War I. It was enough. Congress and many American citizens largely regarded Hitler's conquests as strictly a European problem. "America First" became a popular slogan, and prominent America Firsters included Charles A. Lindbergh, the American hero who in 1927 had flown solo across the Atlantic Ocean to land in Paris.

A few military planners and politicians were deeply concerned about America's isolationism. They realized the airplane had made the world more vulnerable. They felt that a war in Europe might eventually involve America, whether the country liked it or not.

Amelia Earhart

Amelia Mary Earhart was an American aviation pioneer and author who disappeared while flying over the Pacific in 1937. She was attempting an around-the-world flight with her navigator, Fred Noonan. They were flying a twin-engine Lockheed Vega.

In 1932 she became the first woman pilot to fly the Atlantic nonstop. Between 1930 and 1935, Amelia Earhart set seven women's speed and distance records in a variety of aircraft. She made nonstop solo flights from Honolulu to Oakland, California, and from Mexico City to New York City. Earhart participated in long-distance air racing and competed with Jacqueline Cochran—who would later establish the WASPs—in the 1935 Bendix Trophy air race.

Her mysterious disappearance near the Pacific's Howland Island is still controversial. The commonly accepted theory is that she simply ran out of gas and went into the sea. Others are not so sure. One possibility is that she landed on Gardner Island (now called Nikumaroro) and died before she could be rescued. One historian suggests she may have been executed by the Japanese after seeing military installations that had been forbidden by international treaties.

Some American pilots had fought alongside the English and French against the Germans during the First World War. These pilots were part of the US Army, called the Army Air Service. Some women pilots had volunteered to fight but had been turned down. In the 1930s several famous women, including Amelia Earhart and Eleanor Roosevelt, proposed that the US Army incorporate women into the pilot pool.

General Henry "Hap" Arnold was promoted to chief of the air force. It was a flimsy, underfunded service, with fewer than 2,000 aircraft in 1938. Germany had more than double that number. America trained only 300 pilots per year. In the late 1930s the idea of using women pilots had been proposed but was rejected by Arnold because of a lack of airplanes.

There was resistance to an expanded air force by a number of top-ranking generals who believed the military use of aircraft was a fad. Some of these generals still believed in fighting from horseback. Yet there was clear evidence suggesting that aircraft would play a major role in war. Germany showed its air strength to the world when in 1937 it bombed Guernica, a city in Spain, killing hundreds of civilians in the Spanish Civil War. The Japanese use of aircraft in its invasion of China and the devastating bombing of Nanking in 1937 were further proof that air power would be an integral part of future conflicts.

Gertrude was still working for her father at Smooth-On, and like most Americans the first thing she did upon arriving home in the evening was to turn on her radio and listen to the news. As she fixed macaroni and cheese (which she adored) or broiled a chop, she could feel England's desperation through the voice of Edward R. Murrow, an American journalist broadcasting from London as the bombs fell.

World War II and the Draft

When America entered World War II, it needed a lot of soldiers in a hurry, so an involuntary draft was instituted through a system called Selective Service. Men eligible for service were given physicals and were either rejected or deemed fit to fight. President Franklin D. Roosevelt convened a National Nutrition Conference in 1941 to see why 38.5 percent of all men called to serve were rejected. They discovered what welfare workers knew all along: the largest single factor was malnutrition, caused by the Great Depression of the 1930s.

In the autumn of 1940, Gertrude was aware that only the fighter pilots of England's Royal Air Force (RAF) stood between Hitler and an invasion of the British Isles. Hitler's air force, the Luftwaffe, was ordered to destroy the Royal Air Force. Prospects looked bleak for the RAF. Fighting fiercely, the English pilots held the Germans at bay, in spite of heavy losses.

Gertrude asked Henry Silver if he had family in Europe. The word was that the Jews were fleeing the Continent. But contrary to his last name ("Silver" or names with the prefix "Silver-" are common Jewish surnames), Henry was not Jewish. Even so, America had its own ugly streak of anti-Semitism, and kids had teased him in school and called him derogatory names.

Although Henry was still interested in a relationship with Gertrude, her romantic interest was soon firmly directed elsewhere. It was probably at a dance sometime in late 1940 or early 1941 that Gertrude met Stanley Michael (Mike) Kolendorski, the man she would love the rest of her short life.

Mike was a member of Eagle Squadron 71, composed of American pilots who volunteered to fly against the Germans for England. He had returned to the States for an unknown reason and was now waiting for a flight back to England. His destination was his air base at the village of Martlesham Heath, where he piloted a Hurricane, a swift single-engine fighter.

Gertrude and Mike likely found common ground in the fact that they were both from New Jersey. They must have fallen for each other quickly because they spent much of the next several days together. With a war on, romances were often accelerated. Military men had short leaves and would return to duty to face death. One- and two-week romances sometimes ended in proposals of marriage.

Did tearful kisses mark their good-bye as Mike boarded a train for New Hampshire and his flight back to England? Elizabeth was certain that an Eagle Squadron pilot was her sister's "one and only" love, and it is likely the pair fueled their attachment with letters.

News of the war dominated headlines. Moviegoers watched bombs falling and cities in flame. The newsreels showed English fighter planes taking off to meet the Nazi attackers. Gertrude must have worried, for this was a critical time for her Eagle Squadron pilot.

England was bombed intensely for 57 consecutive nights. Eighty thousand Londoners were killed or wounded. A newspaper story estimated 300 English fighter pilots had met their deaths in combat since the war had begun. Called the Battle of Britain, it was the first time a battle was fought using only airplanes.

On the ground, Belgrade had fallen to the Germans, the ninth European capital to capitulate to Hitler. President Roosevelt, while still maintaining America's neutrality, ordered the US Navy and Coast Guard to defend against Nazi submarines attacking ships off America's East Coast. The fires of torpedoed ships were seen from the New Jersey coast.

There is no record of when Gertrude took her first airplane flight, but it is probable that it was with Mike Kolendorski, who rented a plane while he was in New York. After he left for England, she followed up with flying lessons.

Gertrude's first flight must have been exhilarating and life changing, similar to WASP Jean's Hascall Cole's description of her first flight.

My first flight was a stunning introduction to a new world. Bounding along the grass runway, the Aeronca seemed ready to lift at a moment's notice. My feet were on the rudders, one hand on the throttle, one on the stick, carefully following the movements of the instructor who was flying the dual controls from the front cockpit. Suddenly the plane roared into the air, banked to the left, and swept, gloriously, into the deep blue of a clear June sky. This was now my world, this incredibly wide, amazing beautiful new universe.

In May 1941 Gertrude received notification that Pilot Officer Stanley M. Kolendorski had been shot down by the

Germans and was considered dead by the RAF. (Sometime later his body was recovered from the sea, and he was buried in Rockanje, Holland.) The news of Mike's death plunged Gertrude into despair. For two weeks she stayed home from work. She later told her sister that she couldn't stop crying, so she focused on learning to fly.

Six months later, on December 7, 1941, Gertrude listened to the news of the Japanese bombing of Pearl Harbor. Virtually every American found a radio and glued themselves to it on that fateful Sunday morning. The war had finally become personal, and America wasn't ready. It turned to its women for help.

At the war's beginning all military branches began utilizing women. This was something that First Lady Eleanor Roosevelt had been supporting in her My Day newspaper column, which was syndicated in many cities across the United States. The army had the Women's Army Corps (WACs); the navy formed Women Accepted for Volunteer Emergency Services (WAVES); the marine corps had their Women's Reserve; and the coast guard created SPARs from the service's Latin motto, Semper Paratus—Always Ready. All were formed because of shortages of men.

War news monopolized conversation everywhere. There was speculation among female pilots that they might be called upon to fly for their country. Some women pilots got their licenses through Civilian Pilot Training Programs at universities. Many women fliers paid to learn at flight schools scattered across the country. A few women flew professionally, mostly as instructors.

In 1941, about 3,000 American women had pilot's licenses, and many wanted to be of service. Two proposals were submitted to General Hap Arnold, one by Nancy Harkness Love and the other by Jacqueline Cochran. Both were expert pilots, but Cochran was almost a household name. She'd won the Bendix race and five Harmon trophies for her flying and had set many speed, distance, and altitude records. She owned a cosmetics company called Wings and promoted her products by flying around the country and giving interviews. Considered something of an aviation swashbuckler, Jacqueline Cochran had been born Bessie Pittman in 1906 in western Florida, where her handicapped father had sometimes earned 60 cents a day at a sawmill. To escape poverty, Bessie became a hairdresser, and while making her way to New York City, she changed her name to Jacqueline Cochran. Working at the cosmetics counter at Saks Fifth Avenue, she met and later married movie mogul and millionaire Floyd Odlum.

Jacqueline Cochran and Nancy Harkness Love were very different. Love was from a well-to-do family and had an Ivy League college education. While in college she got her pilot's license and made money by renting planes and taking students for rides. She became known as "The Flying Freshman." She and her husband, Robert M. Love, an air corps reserve major, built their own successful Boston-based aviation company, Inter City Aviation, for which Nancy was a pilot. She proposed to the army a small unit of experienced women pilots to ferry aircraft from factories to military bases. Each pilot would have at least 500 hours of flying time. These women already had licenses. Her proposal went to the Air Force Ferry Command.

It was approved, and the Women's Auxiliary Ferrying Squadron (WAFS) was formed under Love. She brought together 28 pilots who met her criteria. They underwent four weeks of specialized military training at New Castle Army Air Base in Delaware. The women learned to fly most of the aircraft in the army and were ready to immediately begin flying.

Unlike Love, Cochran wanted to train large numbers of women to handle all kinds of domestic military flights, thus releasing many more male pilots for combat. While Love's group began ferrying, Cochran was given the go-ahead by General Arnold to organize her training program, the Women's Airforce Service Pilots—the WASPs.

Using word of mouth and personal invitations, Cochran began recruiting. Gertrude was about to embark on her greatest adventure yet.

7

THE WASPs ARE BORN

On September 10, 1942, a *New York Herald Tribune* headline read: WOMEN PILOTS TO FLY FOR ARMY. It was Jacqueline Cochran's announcement of the formation of the Women's Airforce Service Pilots. Gertrude must have seen the article. Like many American women, she had been waiting for this moment.

There were many reasons women chose to apply to the WASPs. Patriotism was at the core, but flying, thanks to the movies, was also considered glamorous. Said WASP Jean Hascall Cole, "For each of us, flying was a passion, and some combination of daring, rebellion, and determination took us into the air."

Like Gertrude, WASP Nadine Nagle's desire to fly for the service was personal. Nagle wrote: "In the summer of 1942 my husband (a B-24 pilot) was killed on a mission in England. I read an article on the women pilots the next month. I got this patriotic feeling that I was to fly in his place."

There was no formal recruitment. Word of mouth and news articles quickly generated 25,000 applications for the WASPs. It happened so quickly that there were few written or regulated standards for admission. Applicants were interviewed by Cochran or one of her assistants. As Molly Merryman writes in her book, "The guidelines were a matter of choosing clean-cut, stable appearing young girls, women who best fit the image of the WASPs as Cochran saw it. . . . We do know that this subjective screening process had a detrimental impact on black women, who Cochran removed from consideration."

Cochran wrote that she feared that admitting African American women to the WASPs would jeopardize the program, saying she had enough difficulty establishing the WASPs and that "it might be the straw that broke the camel's back." Racial discrimination was institutionalized as part of the American military until President Harry S. Truman took the first step to integrate the army in 1947.

However, two Chinese American women were accepted in the program, one of whom, Hazel Ying Lee, later died in a plane crash at Great Falls, Montana. One Native American woman flew for the WASPs, Ola Mildred Rexroat, an Oglala Sioux from the Pine Ridge Indian Reservation in South Dakota.

Gertrude was probably interviewed by Cochran herself in New York City. She met the standards: Caucasian, educated, respectable, and well mannered. Cochran was acutely conscious of the image of her WASPs, and she feared that a misstep by even one of them might be blown up by the press and reflect badly on the program and on her own reputation.

The standards for application in the beginning included a pilot's license and 75 hours of flight time. (In contrast, male applicants for pilot training did not need a pilot's license or any flight experience.) The women's flight time was soon lowered to 35 hours.

Wrote WASP Jean Hascall Cole, "Many of them . . . squeezed in [to the WASP program] by various methods, not all of which were aboveboard. World War II was a very popular war. The country was totally involved and everyone wanted to be 'in it' or helping in one way or another. No holds were barred when it came to 'getting in.'"

WASPs Madeline Sullivan and Jo Wallace were on the way to their entry interview. Neither had the full 35 hours of flying time needed to qualify, but each tried to keep the fact from one another. Madeline asked Jo, "How many hours of signed time do you have [in your pilot's logbook]?" Jo replied she had about 31. Madeline said, "I have news for you. Unless you have 35 hours of signed time, she [Cochran] is not going to put you into the next class in September."

"Oh my God," said Jo. "Have you got a pen?" Both women went into the restroom and finished padding their logbooks. Upstairs, they were both passed for entry into the September class.

One woman with bad vision cheated on her eye exam by squinting. Still another got her doctor to attest that she was taller than the five-foot-two-and-a-half-inch minimum required by the WASPs.

About 1,800 women made the cut and were staged for training. Gertrude Tompkins was one of them.

8

WELCOME TO THE WASPs

The home of the WASPs' 318th Army Air Forces Flying Training Detachment (AAFFTD) was a busy base three miles from downtown Sweetwater, a town of about 10,000 in central Texas. When Gertrude arrived on May 23, 1943, Sweetwater looked to her like a Western movie set. The surrounding countryside was a forlorn-looking landscape where dust swirled in the sparse Texas brush. It had one hotel, the Blue Bonnet, with a corner drugstore that occupied the lower floor of the hotel. There were lots of ranchers and cowboys. They wore jeans, cowboy hats, and cowboy boots with spurs that jingled. The ones with guns on their hips must have presented an impressive sight to the trainees who arrived that day from many cities. The people of Sweetwater were friendly, and the women grew to love them.

From Sweetwater the WASP recruits were driven to
Avenger Field in the "cattle car," a bus-like contraption
towed by a truck. At Avenger Field Gertrude joined WASP
Class 43-W-7 (1943-women-class number 7). There were 103
women in her class at the beginning, each with at least 35
hours flying time (unless they had forged their logbooks).
Each woman had paid her own money to become a flier and
to pass her pilot's test. They'd each paid for their own tickets
to Sweetwater.

As they entered the gates of the base they saw above
them the WASPs' cartoon mascot, Fifinella, or "Fifi," a comic
female gremlin character in flight cap and goggles designed
especially for the women pilots by Walt Disney. Fifi was said
to play pranks on female pilots and could always be blamed
for mischief that was otherwise unexplainable.

As they stood in ranks, an officer strode before them.
"Imagine an empty space where the person is standing next
to you." He waited, letting the women look at one another.
He continued. "About half of you will wash out [fail to meet
training standards]. This program is tough, and if you can't
cut it, you will be asked to pack up and leave."

WASP Alberta Fitzgerald Head wrote about recruits
arriving at Avenger in the winter, "Some thin young shoulders were scantily clad and from the direction of the wind-
whipped pleated skirts we heard a recurrent wail, 'They said
it was warm in Texas!' They wore loafers and high heels,
there were fur coats and sunglasses, plaits and extravagant
hair arrangements. . . . The wind and sand mocked these gal-
lant girls as they entered the ready room [a waiting room of
sorts for pilots] for the first time." Sweetwater could also be
blazing hot. Recruits were herded into a large hall and were

relieved of tennis rackets, musical instruments, high-heeled shoes, and golf clubs, which were shipped home. The first order of business was to swear in the young women. They raised their right hands and took a solemn oath to serve their country. After that, the business of becoming pilots got underway.

Gertrude was 31 years old when she arrived at Sweetwater as part of the 318th Training Detachment, older than most of the recruits. Unlike many of them, she had lived with women roommates at Ambler. She'd traveled extensively and seen the world.

On this breezy May day Gertrude stood proud in the ranks with her class as they formed company 43-W-7. But she was wholly unprepared for the first days of training at Avenger Field. Her face was burned dry by the sun and the wind as she waited for the medics to give her painful inoculations. She was fingerprinted. The flight surgeon made her run in place, then do push-ups and deep knee bends until she was gasping for breath. She learned she had to supply her own washcloth and towels, yet she was quarantined and confined to base.

Six women were assigned to each barrack's bay, and two bays shared a bathroom with showers and toilets. A bay was a room about 20 feet by 20 feet. The latrine (bathroom) windows were clear, and the recruits painted them black to obscure the views of outsiders. The army demanded that the women learn new routines: bunk sheets had to be turned down two hand widths, blankets stretched tight enough to bounce a quarter, shoes placed under the bunk with toes pointing to the center of the bay. On Saturdays they had inspections.

Lights went out at 10:00 PM, and absolute silence was ordered. Each night an officer came through with a flashlight.

WASPs sunbathing between barracks, Avenger Field, Sweetwater, Texas, 1943. *Courtesy of the WASP Archive, Texas Woman's University Libraries*

Once he left, the trainees often gathered in the latrine to play a quiet game of cards and to talk. When the lights went out during winter, so did each bay's gas heater. The card players retired to their bunks after first drawing lots to see who would jump out of her bunk to light the heater in the cold dawn.

The women's assignment to Sweetwater was supposed to be secret, but within days the word was out. Male pilots frequently made "emergency landings" at Avenger. An order from a high-placed officer stopped the male visits, and as a result Avenger Field became known as "Cochran's Convent."

The class of 43-W-7 was separated alphabetically into two flights, or groups. Gertrude was in the second flight. One flight had ground school in the morning and flying time in the afternoon; for the other flight, the schedule was reversed.

For early trainees, the program was 22½ weeks long, with 115 hours of flight training, 20 hours of simulated flight training, 5 hours of physical training each week, and 180 hours of instruction in navigation, communication, weather, aircraft and engines, and Air Transport Command procedures. By the time Gertrude arrived at Avenger Field, her program had been extended to 24 weeks, with 180 hours of flight time and 30 hours of simulated flight training.

Training was in three phases: primary, basic, and advanced. Changes to the program were made constantly. Physical training for the women was increased. Male leaders thought women would need the extra strength to handle the controls of the heavy bombers.

For membership to flight training, the WASPs had requirements to meet and rules to follow that weren't exactly fair, by Gertrude's estimate. The WASPs were a special nonmilitary institution created by Congress and were not covered by the same rules as the other men and women in military services.

The WASP candidates had to be at least 21 years old, but the minimum age for male pilot candidates was only 18. The

Weak Women?

The WASPs flew the biggest and toughest airplanes that the US Army flew in World War II and did so with all the skill of the men, as statistics would later show. The male accident rate for domestic flights in the war was .088 per 1,000 hours flying time. For women, that rate was .060.

Early in its development, the B-29 Superfortress, the giant plane that would drop the atomic bombs on Japan, was rumored by pilot trainees to be balky, difficult, and dangerous to fly. In 1944 Colonel Paul Tibbets selected two WASPs to fly the big plane to different air force bases to show the men it was not a difficult plane to fly. The women would land, get out, and walk around in full view. The men would have second thoughts, either reassured or reproached.

A B-29, the largest bomber of World War II. *Courtesy of the National Museum of the US Air Force*

After the top brass heard about it, Colonel Tibbets was ordered to stop the women from making future flights in the Superfortress. Tibbets was the pilot of the *Enola Gay*, which dropped the first atomic bomb on Hiroshima.

women had to pay their own way to flight school, but the government paid for men to travel to flight training. If the women washed out they had to pay their way back home, while washed-out men were drafted into the army. Women paid $1.65 per day for their room and board; the men got theirs free. The women contributed their own money to an emergency fund for the death or accidental injury of a fellow student; the men each got a $10,000 insurance policy issued by the government. The women had to purchase their uniforms at a cost of at least $100, while the men were provided a uniform allowance of $200, and more for the higher ranks.

Gertrude's pay to start was $150 a month, with $26 paid for overtime; the men were paid only $75 a month while in training but were commissioned second lieutenants with many benefits, which the women were not. After flight training, Gertrude was to be paid a flat $250 a month, but unlike her second lieutenant male counterpart who made $150, she did not get a $21 supplement, $45 for quarters, and $75 flight pay each month, a total of $291.

If she were injured or became ill, she must provide for her own care. (Later, she could pay a fee for use of army hospitals.) The men were provided automatic health care at no personal expense.

And last, ominously, the death benefit for a woman killed in the line of duty was a flat $200 and a plain pine box. There was no military escort, and she wasn't entitled to have the American flag on her coffin. Her family would have no right to a Gold Star, displayed by those who lost a loved one in the war.

Despite the inequalities, the women were proud to be flying for their country and put up with the inequities. There were some silly rules too: in the beginning women trainees were ordered to wear hairnets or turbans. Higher command was concerned about hair becoming tangled in propellers, canopy closing devices, and controls. "We were all so anxious to fly we'd have dyed our hair green, if it had been required," wrote WASP Jean Hascall Cole.

During the early flight classes, the women had no official uniform. Jacqueline Cochran quickly decided that each trainee would purchase, at her own expense, tan cotton gabardine slacks, a long-sleeved white shirt, and a tan overseas cap. (An overseas cap is a like an upside-down boat). Since they were worn during the general's inspections, the pants came to be called "general's pants."

Gertrude had little difficulty with military routine. Her experience at Bergen School and at Ambler had conditioned her for life with other women. But she didn't feel much camaraderie with the younger women, and in her spare time she found herself writing letters and reading. She worried about the possibility that she might have difficulties with her stutter when it came to using the radio. And it is likely she was still grieving over the loss of Mike Kolendorski.

She did well at her morning physical exercise and military drill, and she breezed through classes on maps and charts, weather theory, flight records and logs, parachutes, radio orientation, and more.

She heard lectures on military law and courts-martial and got her lowest scores in training in this subject, a 77. In all other classes she got 80s and 90s. She took notes during intelligence and security classes. The class work went on at length, covering military courtesy, equipment and uniforms, discipline and leadership, command and staff functions, and control tower operations. Over time her courses grew more practical and technical: theory and use of flaps, weather estimating and recording, carburetor ice, hydraulic systems, fuel systems, flight instruments, and electrical systems. Much of this she remembered from her earlier private lessons, and she passed her tests with ease.

Weather, weather, weather. The instructor said, "The plane won't kill you but the weather will." She paid close attention as they entered yet another phase of orientation, this one on fogs, fronts, thunderstorms, turbulence, and electrical storms. She learned about the automatic pilot system, radio compass operations, Morse code, and marker beacons, which helped the pilot to know her aircraft's position along its route. She was issued her first parachute.

Despite her distance from some of the younger women, Gertrude did become close with several of the trainees and earned the affectionate nickname "Tommy" Tompkins. Among her closest friends was Mildred "Mickey" Axton, a bright, vivacious brunette from Kansas. Mickey was married and the mother of a small baby who was being cared for by Mickey's mother while Mickey and her husband, Wayne, flew for their country. Tommy and Mickey would be the only ones in their barracks bay to graduate. Mickey had been licensed to fly since 1940. She left the WASPs in April 1944 when her mother became ill. Mickey applied for a job with Boeing and was hired as a flight test engineer. In May 1944 she became the first woman to fly the huge B-29 Superfortress.

Gertrude's first flights were with an instructor. She had eight hours of flying "dual," with the instructor sitting in the front seat of the open cockpit trainer and the WASP trainee in back.

Morse Code: Talking in Dots and Dashes

Morse code is a series of short and long signals—dots and dashes—that are used to transmit letters of the alphabet as well as numbers. They can be sent by blinking lights, special flag signals, or radio transmission.

The simplest letter in Morse code is e, a single dot. SOS is three dots, three dashes, and three dots, shown this way: ··· − − − ···

Morse code was widely used by the military in World War II. Ships and aircraft communicated using light flashes of Morse, maintaining radio silence so as to not alert the enemy. WASPs could identify airports by the individual signals that were continuously transmitted in Morse code. Morse code was also used to send telegrams and other messages.

Most of their instructors were male. Some were kind and patient, but a few were downright mean. In a dual-control aircraft, when the instructor shoved his control stick back and forth rapidly, the connected control stick in the student's cockpit would hit her knees, said WASP Annelle "Nellie" Henderson. This was referred to as a "stick beating," and there was one particular blond male instructor who did this to Annelle. WASP Jean Hascall Cole saw Nellie's knees afterward. "They were black and blue."

Gertrude Tompkins with parachute and harness during flight training, 1943. *Courtesy of the WASP Archives, Texas Woman's University Libraries*

WASP Jean Moore switched instructors three times in primary training. "My first instructor drank too much." Her second instructor was incompetent and sent her up for a check ride, which is a test of a pilot's skills, before she was ready. As a result, she nearly washed out of the program. Finally, she got "Mr. J. R. Smith, an instructor to instructors. Smith was great."

A few weeks into training the women were allowed their first solo flight. The airplane was usually an open-cockpit Fairchild PT-19 Cornell. Soloing was what they'd been waiting for.

After Gertrude soloed, she began flying cross-country, reading maps and following roads. Cross-country flying presented a unique problem for the women. WASP Ruth Adams recalled that when a female pilot inevitably had to urinate

A PT-19 Cornell. Relatively easy to fly, this was the first plane assigned to Gertrude during her WASP training. *Courtesy of the National Museum of the US Air Force*

during a long flight, she had to somehow shed her "great big fleece-lined leather jacket," then "a big fleece-lined leather overall," her flight suit, and "some kind of winter underwear." Once she managed to get all that off, she had to "scoot over to the edge of her seat to where she could pee without getting it on to anything. Then she got all this paraphernalia back onto herself and never got off course."

Aerobatics were part of airplane handling, and the women started by learning gently curving, rolling, climbing, and descending maneuvers called lazy eights, Immelman turns, and chandelles. A glance at the sky over Sweetwater revealed a dozen maneuvering aircraft at any moment, each one neatly recovering from spins and stalls and zooming off to do it again. Gertrude loved the advanced aerobatics, such as snap rolls, half rolls, and slow rolls.

Fellow trainee Jane Tallman posted a menu of maneuvers in the ready room:

```
Slow rolls (plain) ------------------------------ .05
Slow rolls (with whipped cream) ---------------- .15
Half rolls -------------------------------- free
Snap rolls ---------------------------------- .25 up
```

On their early solo flights, some of the trainees got lost and had to land on ranches or farms. They called the base to be picked up. Others navigated their flights by noting the town names on the water towers.

They were all shaken by the first accident they witnessed. During primary training, WASP Margaret Oldenburg had lifted off in a PT-19 and crashed within seconds. Since the crash was close to the end of the runway, many of the women got to look at the plane after the pilot was taken to the hospital. The engine was in the cockpit, both wings were torn off, and the tail assembly was ripped away. Flying is serious business, the instructing supervisor warned, and he wondered aloud if women were up to it. Later investigation would discover that the plane was "out of rig" (i.e., the plane's maneuvering surfaces—the rudder on the tail and the flaps on the wings—were not synchronized), and flight restrictions had been placed on it before Margaret took it up.

Some of the men on the base were openly hostile to the women. That a man might purposely expose a female pilot to danger seemed unthinkable. But rumors of sabotage swept the Sweetwater ready room: a disgruntled aircraft factory

A WASP instructor and trainee, Avenger Field, Sweetwater, Texas.
Courtesy WASP Archives, Texas Woman's University Libraries

Sabotage? Really.

Several WASP accounts are firm about their aircraft being sabotaged. After having to parachute from an out-of-control BT-13, WASP Lorraine Zilner learned her rudder cables had been cut partway through. WASP Mary Ellen Keil had a fire start from an oily rag left in an AT-6 engine; during another takeoff attempt, all the flight controls came loose from the side of her airplane. "I don't think it was anything but sabotage," she said. "Nobody could be so careless."

"The stories of sabotage seemed unlikely to many of us, but the possibility was taken very seriously by the girls who had encountered unexplained, serious damage to their aircraft," wrote WASP Jean Hascall Cole in *Women Pilots of World War II*.

employee was reportedly pulling up grass and stuffing it in fuel tanks; there were crossed fuel lines and coolant lines; sugar was supposedly poured in aviation fuel; tires were said to have been expertly slashed so as to blow out not on takeoff but on landing; there was a rumor of a parachute wrapped with a loosely corked vial of acid inside.

The women were told to double-check their equipment, planes, and engines. Some of them were sure that a few men on the base wanted the women to fail.

The male officers made the women switch from hair-nets to turbans, concerned that the women's long hair might

WASPs of class 43-W-7 taking a break on a PT-19 during primary training. The WASP Archives at Texas Women's University identifies Gertrude Tompkins as being on the far left, leaning on the wing, wearing
dark glasses and saddle oxfords. The family believes that Gertrude is
at the top of the picture with her arm leaning on the fuselage. *Courtesy
of WASP Archives, Texas Woman's University Libraries*

become tangled in the controls of their aircraft. Gertrude's
hair was short, but even so, she was required to wear the tur-
ban. Although turbans were popular in the 1940s, for female
pilots they were a nuisance and were hated by most of them.

Meanwhile, Jacqueline Cochran was getting reports
on trainee performance. The reports said that the women

needed more instruction on the "whiz wheel," a circular slide rule used by aviators before modern technology provided easier means of navigating. They also needed more training in crosswind landings. There were too many ground loops. A ground loop is when a plane does a spin after landing, often caused by crosswinds. The report also said the trainees did not have enough cross-country flying instruction, and they lacked knowledge about group flying and formation flying. What's more, they knew little about military customs and courtesies.

After primary training, Gertrude left the PT-19 behind and moved on to the next phase, basic training.

9

BASIC AND ADVANCED TRAINING

Some things remained unchanged after moving up to basic training: the classrooms, the marching, the calisthenics, as well as cleaning the barracks, washing clothes, and answering letters. But there was one big difference. Gertrude would now take the controls of the infamous BT-13, a 440-horsepower single-engine plane made by the Vultee Aircraft Corporation. Nicknamed the "Vultee Vibrator," it was also referred to as a bucket of bolts. It had a bad reputation. The BT-13s the women trained in were old, rattling, shaky, and, as Gertrude found out soon enough, unreliable in spins.

WASP Lorraine Zilner had a particularly bad experience in a BT-13, she recalled, when "all of a sudden the plane just went completely out of control and flipped into an inverted spin. I stayed with it, I worked with it, I did everything possible. I stayed with it as long as I could, and then I tried to get out. . . . My chute had just barely opened when I hit the ground. . . . That was the end of that airplane."

The BT washed out a dozen less-capable women in 43-W-7, and the airplane eventually killed nine WASPs in accidents.

But Gertrude's greatest fear in flying the BT was that she now would be required to speak using the radio. Her primary training plane had only an intercom between instructor and trainee. In the BT, radio communication with the control tower was required. She had to call before taxiing out to the runway, had to call the tower for flight instructions, and had to call the tower again for landing instructions.

Gertrude worked very hard to memorize her calls and control her stutter, speaking slowly and distinctly. She may have sung her radio procedures, said her friend and fellow

WASPs pray to the BT-13 for luck, Avenger Field, Sweetwater, Texas. They disliked flying the unpredictable and sometimes dangerous training plane. *Courtesy WASP Archives, Texas Woman's University Libraries*

WASP Mickey Axton. She did not stutter when singing. In any event her instructors gave her passing marks.

Once aloft, despite being wary of the BT-13, she felt thrilled at the privilege of being allowed to fly planes that were off-limits to the public.

Film and the 1940s

The WASPs' favorite off-duty pastime was watching movies. Americans were riding a wave of patriotism generated by filmmakers in response to Pearl Harbor. By 1942 war films dominated the silver screen, with *Casablanca*, *Wake Island*, *Mrs. Miniver*, and *Eagle Squadron* being big at the box office. In 1943, 13 of the top 20 box office films were about the war. A year later, Americans still watched war movies, such as *Thirty Seconds over Tokyo*, *Since You Went Away*, and *Hollywood Canteen*. In 1944, when fears eased and America appeared to be winning the war, many moviegoers went to see less combative fare such as *Going My Way*, *Gaslight*, *National Velvet*, and *Meet Me in St. Louis*. But the subject of war didn't disappear entirely from popular films: in 1946, *The Best Years of Our Lives*, a story of homecoming veterans, won nine Academy Awards, including Best Motion Picture.

Most World War II war movies are today scorned by film critics as propagandistic, although *Casablanca* is considered a classic.

Planning cross-country flights on the wing of an AT-6 Texan. The women loved the swift little advanced trainer, and Gertrude made her cross-country solo flight in a Texan. *Courtesy of the WASP Archive, Texas Women's University Libraries*

If Gertrude had mixed feelings about the BT-13, she soon reveled in flying the heavenly AT-6 Texan. Quick, powerful, maneuverable, and fun to fly, the AT-6 was a favorite among training pilots. Gertrude dashed through each morning's end-of-class tests so she could be in the cockpit sooner.

In pilot's lingo, the plane "lifted off hot," meaning it rose quickly under her touch. It seemed to ride the skies with silken ease. The AT-6 had a covered cockpit like a greenhouse, and as the morning sun climbed higher over the Texas plains Gertrude pushed back the canopy, allowing in a little air. She felt thrilled as she pierced a cloud, and marveled as she dived at more than 200 miles an hour. She felt the hot beams of the sun on her neck before heading for home at Avenger Field. After she landed, she told her friend Mickey she felt Mike's love up there.

While Gertrude handled real airplanes with ease, she met her match in the Link trainer. The Link was a hooded black box inside which the women handled simulated controls. It trained them for night and bad weather flying. Gertrude had developed excellent flying habits, but inside the Link she

Class 43-W-7 forming up to march. They are wearing the oversized men's "zoot suits" provided by an army air force unprepared for women pilot trainees. Gertrude Tompkins is in the middle of the group, looking slightly down. *Courtesy WASP Archives, Texas Woman's University Libraries*

kept insisting on using her instincts when she should have relied on her instruments. After her first session in the Link she emerged fearful and drenched in sweat. The instructor failed her. She was acutely aware that almost half the class had washed out for one reason or another, and she was afraid the Link would cause her own failure.

Her friend Mickey came to the rescue. Having flown since she was 11, Mickey excelled at instrument work. The pair spent hours practicing in the Link, with Mickey gently telling Gertrude to "let go of what you feel, and let the instruments think for you." Gertrude passed her 15 hours of training in the Link. She was never comfortable with night flying, and she was grateful the WASPs were required to land their ships before sunset and remain overnight (RON) wherever they were.

As their skills improved, class 43-W-7 concentrated on cross-country flights, frequently to Harpersville, Texas, some 200 miles from Sweetwater. To rouse herself after long, boring stretches, Gertrude might turn the plane over and fly upside down for a while, amusing herself by keeping the compass on a perfect heading directed to her destination. If she'd been caught doing this, she might have been washed out. But a hundred miles from Sweetwater, who would ever know? At night, as they lay in bed after lights out, the women shared their secrets, and when Gertrude told them about flying upside down the place erupted in laughter.

She anticipated with excitement her longest cross-country flight in the AT-6. After she dressed, she plotted her course from Sweetwater. Her destination was Blythe, California. Setting the brakes, Gertrude revved up her engine and looked back at the billowing dust kicked up, enveloping the planes behind her. She released the brakes, and the plane practically

Trainees learn about the "whiz wheel," a calculating device used to navigate over long distances. *Courtesy WASP Archives, Texas Woman's University Libraries*

leaped off the ground to become airborne. The flight took her across south-central Texas and into New Mexico. She crossed the Rocky Mountains, where peaks were dusted with November snow and the aspen fields stood out ghostly white while the pines looked almost black. To Gertrude's left was the Rio Grande River and Mexico. Up high like this she could see the Rockies marching north toward Canada. She landed and returned uneventfully.

Some of the army air force men were saying women shouldn't be flying while having their menstrual periods. For a while there had been an edict banning women from flying while they were menstruating. "None of us ever has a period, as a result," Gertrude told Elizabeth. Since all the women lied about it, Jackie Cochran convinced Hap Arnold, general of the air force, that the rule was nonsense. Besides, the women had real dangers to worry about. As 1943 progressed and more women were flying, deaths among the WASPs were mounting.

Cornelia Fort, a Tennessean who'd been instructing in a Piper Cub over Hawaii when the Japanese bombed Pearl Harbor, was killed in a collision on March 21 when a show-off male pilot tried to do a slow roll around her BT-13 near Merkel, Texas.

Margaret Oldenburg, class of 43-4, plunged into a farmer's field near Houston in a PT-19 Cornell on March 7. At the hospital an attendant was told off by Margaret's waiting classmates when he described her face as being "pulverized to jelly."

Jane Champlin was killed June 3 in a nighttime BT-13 crash near Westbrook, Texas. She had written to a friend that she didn't trust her instructor, who was known to sleep while in flight, and he was with her at the time of the crash. The watch that was taken from her wrist had stopped on impact at 11:15.

Kathryn Lawrence, a trainee in the class following Gertrude's, was killed on August 3 near Sweetwater when her PT-19 spun in.

Margaret Selph and Helen Severson collided near Big Spring, Texas, on August 30, and both were killed.

Pilot error accounted for most accidents, with mechanical failure next, and then weather.

On November 19, 1943, Gertrude and her class of 43-W-7 graduated to the march tunes of the Big Spring Bombardier School Band. Dressed in light tan general's pants, a white blouse, and a cocked overseas cap, she received her silver wings, pinned on by Mrs. Barton K. Yount, wife of Lieutenant General Barton K. Yount, commanding general of the army air force flying training center. Only 59 of Gertrude's original 103 classmates graduated.

Each class sang its own distinctive song as they passed in review. Gertrude sang:

> *W seven is winning the war, parley voo*
> *W seven is winning the war, parley voo*
> *W seven is winning the war,*
> *To hell with six and five and four*
> *Hinky-dinky parley-voo!*

Gertrude's class, 43-W-7, in formation preparing to march in the graduation ceremony. Gertrude, with short dark hair, is in the center of the group, looking slightly down. *Courtesy of the WASP Archive, Texas Woman's University Libraries*

10

PECOS

Gertrude had applied for the air force fighter pilot school conducted at Brownsville, Texas, but upon graduation from advanced training her orders sent her to the army air base in Pecos, Texas, instead.

She was pleased to be assigned to be a test pilot in AT-6 Texans, the same plane she had flown and adored in advanced training. She loved the power and speed of the little Texan, and she wanted more. She held out hope that soon she would be assigned to fly the fastest single-engine fighter planes, then called pursuit planes. Some of them were three times more powerful than the AT-6.

Other members of her graduating class would tow target banners far behind their planes, providing gunners on the ground with marksmanship practice. Most would be ferrying planes wherever they were needed: bombers to the east and west coasts and trainers to various air bases. Some women would fly transports and light aircraft for military officers. Gertrude embraced her flying life with enthusiasm and was pleased to learn Mickey Axton would join her at Pecos flying AT-6s.

At about this time, Gertrude's friend Henry Silver, who hadn't given up on winning her over, told Gertrude that her father wanted Henry to join Smooth-On Company after the war ended. Gertrude was aware from her father's letters how much Vreeland liked Henry. It felt like her father loved Henry like the son he and Laura had lost in childbirth. But according to Elizabeth, Gertrude may also have felt like Henry was operating behind her back.

A WASP at the controls of an AT-6 Texan. Gertrude was a test pilot of AT-6s after being assigned to Pecos army air base. *Courtesy of the WASP Archive, Texas Women's University Libraries*

But Gertrude would have had little time to worry about Henry Silver. Pecos Army Air Base kept her in the air and very busy. Here the men of the air force were being trained to become pilots, and Gertrude's job as part of Flight 17B was to test aircraft to be sure they were safe. Several times each

America's Industrial Might

In 1939 America's air force had only 2,000 airplanes. By the time of Pearl Harbor's bombing on December 7, 1941, America was already increasing military aircraft production. In 1942, 47,800 planes were built. In 1943 the number jumped to 86,000. By war's end in 1945, America had built 296,429 warplanes.

As America assembled a 12 million-man army, the country turned to its corporations. More than 2,700 large cargo ships, called Liberty ships, were built. The record time to construct one, the SS *Robert E. Peary*, was just four days, 15 hours, and 29 minutes. Chrysler made tanks instead of cars. Ford's huge Willow Run plant turned out one B-24 Liberator bomber every hour. General Motors built everything from airplanes to machine guns.

For millions of Americans the war was a financial bonanza, providing jobs and money and bringing down the curtain on the Great Depression. It gave rise to women in the workplace, and Rosie the Riveter, the symbol of working factory women during the war, became an American icon.

day she climbed into AT-6s, either new or recently repaired, and put them through their paces. She took off, flew a tight course of turns, then stalled and dived them, testing out various maneuvers and spins.

"If the wings stay on and the engine still runs," then she would certify it, she told Elizabeth, who was now living in Southern Pines, North Carolina. She had returned to America from Egypt, leaving her husband in his job in the war-torn Middle East.

She was joking with her sister. In truth, Gertrude was diligent in her work. She frequently refused to certify planes that she felt were dangerous. She had flown in too many substandard planes at Sweetwater, and she made a nuisance of herself agitating for new planes for the male student pilots at Pecos.

The dust in Pecos was worse than in Sweetwater, and the base was alive with nearly 5,000 officers, enlisted men, and trainees who took lessons in the planes she tested. About 200 Women's Army Corps (WAC) administrators and secretaries and another 23 WASPs were the only women on the base.

During their time in Pecos, Gertrude and Mickey took up wearing Ray-Bans, the dark glasses made famous by aviators. They were lucky to get them. The Christmas of 1943 was meager all over America. A rationing system had been put in place by the government. There were no outdoor decorative lights, and tinsel for Christmas tree decorations was unavailable. There were no turkeys or cranberries, and sliced bread was almost impossible to find (the metal used in slicing machines was going to war production). Butter and whipping cream were impossible to buy. Beef and gasoline were sold on the black market. Silk stockings were unavailable. You couldn't buy elastic anywhere, and Gertrude was glad she still had silk underwear from before the war. Bobby pins were gone. Radios had virtually disappeared from the shelves. Metal, rubber, chemicals, and food were all going overseas to help fight the war.

Although she was busy, and good at her work, Gertrude's stay at Pecos seemed interminable because she anticipated being reassigned. Each morning in the mess hall there was war talk. Big news came on June 6, 1944, when the invasion of France by Allied troops—D-day—was announced. Many thought the war would be over by Christmas. Gertrude must have wondered what that meant for her future.

The Paperback Book Goes to War

During the Depression, 19 out of 20 books cost $2 or more and were too expensive for most Americans. In 1939 Pocket Books and Penguin Books introduced paperback titles at 25 cents a book.

In the middle of World War II, in 1943, publishers decided to practically give away 122 million paperback books to American military men and women with the idea of enlarging the reading market. The proposal by the Council of Books in Wartime to sell paperbacks to the military for six cents each initially worried some publishers. The military then gave them free to fighting units all over the world.

America embraced the paperback, and today it provides the single most popular form of book reading.

11

ON SILVER WINGS

After about one month in Pecos, orders arrived assigning Gertrude to pursuit school. There she would learn to fly pursuit, or fighter, planes. She did an impromptu dance with fellow WASP Mickey Axton. No more dusty Pecos. She was assigned officially to Fifth Ferry Group, headquartered at Love Field in Dallas, but was ordered to detach to Brownsville and the army's "top gun" training school, where only the best male pilots were sent prior to combat. There were only four other women in her class. She reported on August 15, 1944, and the lineup of powerful fighter planes she saw took her breath away: Thunderbolts, Lightnings, Mustangs. Even the names were thrilling.

Her first day in class she noticed a freckled young pilot smiling at her. His name was Duncan Miller. He was 10 years younger than Gertrude and had a charming, wisecracking sense of humor. One of the first nights Gertrude was in Brownsville, Duncan knocked on the door of her barracks and introduced himself. Brash and full of his ability to fly airplanes, he came right out and said she was pretty and had an "ooh-la-la figure," and that he wanted to take her out on a date.

Duncan said of Gertrude, "She had a great personality. Really a sharp girl. Any time off we probably spent together. I went to Matamoros [in Mexico, just across the border from Brownsville] with her a few times. We walked around, sometimes with two or three other guys and a couple of gals. I sat on her barracks steps with her in the evening, just talking. At night we listened to the radio and danced sometimes. We were in separate quarters. Just four WASPS and the rest were men, so there was pretty heavy competition."

Duncan said Gertrude "was considered a good pilot. If you weren't good you didn't make it. One out of four died in our class," he said, referring to the many pursuit pilots who went on to combat or who died in domestic accidents.

The pair enjoyed spending time together. They went to an on-base movie and shared a Coke. Perhaps this young flier made Gertrude realize that she had options besides Henry.

But Gertrude's main enchantment at the time was aeronautic, not romantic. Her assigned plane in Brownsville thrilled her. It was a P-51D Mustang, its shiny aluminum finish shimmering in the Texas sun. It was rated at speeds over 400 miles an hour. The model was the latest in this line of remarkable fighter planes.

The instructors at Brownsville were emphatic about three-point landings in the Mustang. This meant that as Gertrude approached the landing strip, the instructors wanted the

Music and World War II

With the boys away, the girls at home turned their radios to sentimental songs such as "I'll Walk Alone" and "Don't Sit under the Apple Tree (With Anyone Else But Me)." The songs from the 1943 Broadway musical *Oklahoma!* were everywhere: "Oh, What a Beautiful Mornin'" and "People Will Say We're in Love."

But it was a skinny kid from Hoboken, New Jersey, who changed the music of the war years. On the night of December 30, 1942, Frank Sinatra began singing at New York's Paramount Theatre and a girl swooned. Another stood up and screamed. In seconds every girl in the theater was on her feet screaming. The legend of the crooner was born. The military men overseas resented him. Sinatra seemed to have won over all their sweethearts.

nose of the plane up slightly, so that three points—both front wheels and the tail wheel—kissed the earth at the same time. If the powerful fighter landed on its front wheels first, it had a tendency to do a dangerous, uncontrolled rotation, called a ground loop. "Once you could do a three-point [landing], they opened the candy store," Gertrude wrote to her sister.

Her first walk-around of the new Mustang D model took Gertrude's breath away. Its long, air-cooled engine enabled designers to carve sleek lines from its pointed nose to its square tail. The plane's deep belly scoop seemed to lend it a muscular toughness. A new-model four-bladed propeller hub was streamlined into its nose. Aviation historians agree that the Mustang D is one of the most beautiful airplanes ever built, and it is considered a major factor in winning World War II.

The Mustang saw combat in both the European and the Pacific theaters of war. It was very fast and maneuverable, and its 1,500-mile range enabled the pilot to escort bombers on their missions deep into the heart of enemy territory. Mustang pilots engaged enemy fighters attacking the bombers. Early in the war in Europe, bomber losses were high. But with the Mustang and other fighters escorting and protecting the bombers, losses dropped significantly. Of course Gertrude would be transporting the fantastic plane, not fighting in it, but she was just as thrilled to get behind the wheel.

Gertrude settled into the cockpit and touched the levers and toggles of the D model. She loved the clear bubble canopy,

A P-51 D, about 1,500 horsepower and considered one of the finest combat airplanes of all time. *Courtesy of the National Museum of the US Air Force*

The Mustang Today

Although replaced by jet planes, the P-51 Mustang continued in service in the United States until well after World War II. It saw combat again during the Korean War, from 1950 to 1953. The Mustang was in service in other countries until 1984.

There are a quite a few Mustangs still in operation. They are frequent winners at air races, two of the most popular racers being planes called "Voodoo" and "Strega." There are many Mustangs in museums, and air shows frequently feature them.

Some 15,100 Mustangs came off the production lines during World War II. The cost to build each plane was $51,000. After the war some of them were sold to friendly nations under a reciprocal treaty for one dollar each. Working Mustangs sell today for $2 million to $4 million, depending on condition.

with its unimpeded 360-degree view. She ticked off the cautions of her instructors: Look out for torque—the twist caused by the power and direction of the propeller. Directional stability could be a problem due to a gas tank installed behind the pilot. Never forget to taxi in an S formation, because the high nose blocked the pilot's vision of the runway ahead. Expect blackouts when pulling out of dives. Blackouts occur when gravity forces pull blood from the brain. The pilot becomes momentarily unconscious until the plane comes out of its dive and the blood returns. When taking off, be sure to put the throttle to full power; there had been some engine failures reported at lower power.

Thundering into the sky, she lifted the wheels using a hand crank in the cockpit. She swiftly climbed above the Texas landscape. Gertrude first practiced flying straight and level to get a feel for the Mustang's handling. Once away from Brownsville, she executed various rolls. After that she stalled the plane, surprised at how it wanted to climb, then dropped in high-speed spins that left her thrilled and laughing.

Throttled-up, she blazed across Boca Chica Beach a hundred feet off the ground, scattering gulls and pelicans. She thundered across the Gulf of Mexico and sliced into the towering clouds. Reluctantly, after an hour, she returned to touch down on the airstrip at Brownsville. She found that landing was easier than in the AT-6. There was less likelihood of "swapping ends," or doing a ground loop.

Several hours later Duncan Miller said, "Your stutter. It's gone."

And so it was. A speech impediment that had bedeviled Gertrude for 30 years had fled during her first flight in a Mustang. It would never return. What must her thoughts have been?

On silver wings Gertrude Tompkins discovered herself. The ox that had stood on her tongue for so long had vanished during her first flight in a Mustang, left behind somewhere in the clouds. Elizabeth later agreed that Gertrude's newfound self-confidence came as a gift from the sky.

Gertrude racked up hours in the Mustang during the day. She received the same training that combat pilots underwent and practiced aerial dogfighting with other trainees. There are tales of WASP pilots ferrying fighters engaging in mock dogfights with navy pilots in swift Corsairs and army pilots in powerful Thunderbolts. (When a WASP tells the story, the women always win.) In the evenings and on weekends Gertrude enjoyed spending time with Duncan. In Matamoros they bought a big Mexican sombrero and trinkets, laughed together, talked about flying, and kissed sometimes.

This happy, carefree time was interrupted when Gertrude got a telephone call from Henry Silver, now in the army and based in New York. His tone was subdued and serious. The year before, Henry's sister Margaret had died after giving birth to a daughter. The girl, named Ann, was now nearly a

Beauty Is a Duty

American women were encouraged by cosmetics advertisers to look pretty for the morale of the country during wartime. Hair was typically shoulder length. A popular hairstyle was called the Victory Roll, said to represent an enemy aircraft spiraling down to destruction. Hair turbans and snoods became popular. Courage Red and Victory Red were both lipstick colors of the era. Brown gravy applied to the legs suggested nylon stockings. Fitted military-style jackets and tailored skirts or slacks were popular with women. Teens were beginning to wear jeans with untucked dress shirts and rolled-down socks. Teenage girls were called bobby-soxers.

year old. The father was unknown, Henry said uncomfort-
ably. The baby had been cared for by family friends, but it was
time that she found a permanent home. Henry asked Gertrude to marry him and to be Ann's mother.

Gertrude felt like she was being manipulated, especially
after she got a letter from Vreeland a few days later, in
which he emphasized what he felt was an important point.
If Gertrude adopted the girl, her father pointed out, her new
daughter would not "carry the inherited burden of our stutter." Vreeland also reminded Gertrude that she was now 32
years old, and if she wanted a husband the time was passing quickly. Finally, he wrote how much he and her mother
liked Henry and that if Gertrude married him he would be
warmly welcomed into the family. She was being asked to
choose between loyalty to her father and a career in flying.

Gertrude did not give Henry or her father an immediate
answer.

12

FLYING FOR HER COUNTRY

Though it must have weighed heavily on her mind, Gertrude didn't let her dilemma of whether or not to marry Henry affect her work. She graduated from fighter school in Brownsville and was given her coveted white card, which meant she would be among the 126 WASPs who flew the fastest and most powerful single-engine American fighter planes. And she would be ferrying P-51s.

By 1944 about half of the WASP graduates were ferrying airplanes. Coast-to-coast flights could take several days, depending on the weather and on how fast the plane flew. The day of a WASP ferry pilot was long and unpredictable. At some bases a WASP might not know what type of plane she would be flying the next day—a multiengine bomber or smaller planes, such as Piper Cubs and liaison aircraft.

For Gertrude, ferrying Mustangs offered a vagabond's life. While Dallas's Love Field and the Fifth Ferry Group was her official base and her footlockers were there, she seldom stayed at Love. Most of the time she was either in the air or waiting to pick up a new Mustang from the North American manufacturing plant in Los Angeles. When waiting to take delivery of a plane, she stayed with the Sixth Ferry Group WASPs stationed in Long Beach. On flight days she would take a military bus from Long Beach to the North American

"Follow Me!" From left: WASPs May Ball, Jana Crawford, and Mary Estill head for a P-51 at Scott Army Air Base in Gary, Indiana, 1944.
Courtesy of the WASP Archive, Texas Woman's University Libraries

plant 20 miles north. If there was any place she called home during those hectic months, it was the cockpit of a Mustang.

Weather could extend her trips east. It often took three days to deliver a plane to an Eastern port city. One night she might stay over in Phoenix and the next in Raleigh-Durham, North Carolina. After delivery, she flew back to Los Angeles by hitching a ride on a westbound military plane. She also had clearance to bump military men, even generals, from commercial flights, and sometimes she did. When she arrived in Los Angeles there was always another Mustang to be flown east. After a night's rest, she was off again. She was free of regimentation and on her own. She loved every minute of it.

A WASP reporting to the ferrying flight line looked at the board to see what plane she'd been assigned and its point of delivery. Then she planned her route and her RONs—the places she would land to remain overnight.

Besides ferrying, WASPs oriented pilots returning from overseas to new aircraft models and to the latest technical innovations. Some WASPs also trained radio operators to use the latest equipment and procedures. Some flew low-level night missions, dropping flares on troop training positions and gun emplacements. WASPs flew planes to check the weather, and they flew for bombardier schools and flight engineering tests. WASPs flew hospital planes. They taught instructors how to teach new pilots. They flew attack feints to train combat pilots. They were at the controls of administrative flights involving high military and government officials.

Towing large cloth target banners that were fired at by gunners using live ammunition was another WASP assignment, and it could be dangerous. Mabel Rawlinson was a graduate of 43-W-3 on duty towing targets for army antiaircraft gunnery practice. She was shot down by friendly fire on August 23, 1944, at Camp Davis, North Carolina. They heard her cries when they tried to pull her from the burning wreckage. She died later in a hospital.

Some WASPs helped Russia fight the war. It is possible that Gertrude was among those who delivered P-39 Airacobras and P-63 King Cobras from the Bell Aircraft Corporation in Buffalo, New York, to Great Falls, Montana. There they

Ferrying Airplanes

Airplane ferrying had been the main reason the air force wanted women to fly. Planes produced in the United States had to be flown from factories for deliveries to ports of embarkation and at other places in the country, as well as to Canada. A plane delivered to a port would be partially dismantled and placed in a protective cover before it was put aboard a ship for transport to a theater of the war.

By the time the WASPs were disbanded, they had delivered 12,652 airplanes to bases all over the United States. By 1944 WASPs "were ferrying the majority of all pursuit planes and were so integrated into the Ferry Division that their disbandment caused delays in pursuit deliveries," wrote Molly Merryman in *Clipped Wings*.

During their brief existence, WASPs flew more than 60 million hours in America's defense.

P-51Ds in formation. *Courtesy of the National Museum of the US Air Force*

would then be taken by both male and female Russian pilots to Alaska. After refueling, the Russians flew them across the Bering Sea to bases in the Soviet Union. The P-39 was highly regarded in Russia, where it scored more aerial combat victories than any other plane used by the Soviets against the Germans. WASP Hazel Ying Lee, flying a P-63 King Cobra, was killed in a crash at Great Falls delivering this plane to the Russians.

Byrd Howell Granger, author of *On Final Approach*, wrote of a meeting between a male pilot and a WASP in Great Falls. The young man seemed impressed by the Russian women, waiting in their baggy suits to pick up P-39s to fly to Russia: "Say, now, have you seen those Russian women pilots? Aren't they really something?"

A very tired WASP, hunched over on her heels with her back against a wall, thought: *Who do you think flew the darned things here?* This same WASP flew the route from Buffalo to Great Falls often, and sometimes she gave lipsticks to the Russian women. "Don't speak the same language, but our smiles speak just the same," wrote Granger.

WASP Anne Noggle (44-W-1) wrote in her book *A Dance with Death,* "All WASPs wondered how we would fare if we were called upon to fly in combat. We talked about it in our barracks during our six months of flight training. . . . Our questions and speculation were purely hypothetical."

For some women, combat was not hypothetical at all. Russian women are credited for being the first women to fly in combat. Russian women had a long tradition of serving alongside men as warriors. The legendary Amazons were a tribe of women who dominated the south of Russia during ancient times. During the Bolshevik revolution of 1917, one of the best-known fighting groups was the Women's Battalion of Death.

In Russia, women pilots had a very different experience during World War II than American WASPs. From the first days of Russia's invasion by Germany in June 1941, more than 1,000 Soviet women pilots climbed into cockpits and fought ferociously. They frequently shot down superior-performing German planes. They created mayhem by bombing and strafing ground troops. Many Russian women pilots were killed in combat.

In America, although not engaged in combat, WASPs were gaining respect and lustrous reputations as they fulfilled their duties. Hundreds of letters of commendation and favorable reports came from every station where WASPs operated. The Air Medal was given to Women's Air Ferry Service founder

Nancy Harkness Love. Jackie Cochran was presented with the Distinguished Service Medal.

General Hap Arnold wrote that their "very successful record of accomplishment has proved that in any future total effort the nation can count on thousands of its young women to fly any of its aircraft."

Along with her own growing mastery of all types of planes and assignments, the glowing reputation of the WASPs must have made Gertrude feel proud and confident, and made her decision about marriage that much harder.

13

DILEMMA

There was another factor that influenced the decision Gertrude was about to make regarding Henry Silver's proposal to marry and to become the mother to his infant niece. Surprisingly, there was a growing movement to disband the WASPs.

From the beginning the WASPs were civilians and thus different from all other women's branches of the military. They were formed under the army air force but were the only women's military branch established during World War II that did not have congressional approval.

"I had expected militarization [becoming an official military branch] and looked forward to becoming part of the Air Corps," said WASP Nadine Nagle, who joined in honor of her dead husband. WASP Clarice Bergemann said, "I thought I was in the military and I was surprised when I was told that it

WASP Louesa F. Thompson (43-W-6) preparing for flight in a swift twin-engined P-38. *Courtesy of WASP Archive, Texas Woman's University Libraries*

was civil service." The women joined the air force expecting to receive air force pay; funds to cover hospitalization, housing, and living expenses; and the other benefits afforded to military service members.

The women were trained to meet and perform all the standards required of members of the military. WASPs had to follow military customs and procedures; they wore uniforms and were instructed in drill and military courtesy. In the expectation of being militarized, some were sent to the air force Officer Candidate School in Orlando, Florida.

There was at least one proposal to place the WASPs under the Women's Army Corps, the WACs, headed by Oveta Culp

Hobby, the woman Jackie Cochran had clashed with and said she "loved to hate."

Both Nancy Harkness Love and Jackie Cochran had submitted proposals for militarization, but the proposals were turned down. By 1944 the conflict over militarization of the WASPs grew and intensified. By late summer of that year the American military had moved swiftly through France and was at Germany's border. Many predicted the war in Europe would be over by Christmas (Germany actually would fight fanatically until May 8, 1945).

Many in Congress felt that it was acceptable for women to be in auxiliaries "as stenographers, telephone operators and stewardesses" but that women in the military might lead to women in combat. Several members of Congress were concerned that women in the military would "insult society women who were volunteering in the war effort because they would have attractive uniforms."

Another congressman asked the army, "You are going to start a matrimonial agency, aren't you?" The army replied that in World War I and so far in World War II there had never been a problem with nurses marrying soldiers. Another congressman was concerned that women officers might give orders to men in the regular army.

Some voices were raised in support of women in the military: "Are we to deny the patriotic, courageous women of America the opportunity of participating in this war?" asked one congressman.

Leading the push to disband the WASPs were many of the newer male pilots. Because of its vast training programs, America had more male pilots than airplanes by 1944. Some of these pilots were fearful of being assigned to the infantry as America advanced against Germany and Japan. The men's lobbying resulted in a negative campaign against the WASPs in the media and Congress, a campaign that found many supporters because of the cultural belief of male superiority and privilege.

The columnist Drew Pearson had begun to make an issue of women pilots "taking the jobs of men pilots." Pearson railed against "[General Hap] Arnold's efforts to sidetrack law by continuing to use WASPs while more than 5,000 trained men pilots, each with an average of 1,250 flying hours, remain idle."

A 1944 publicity shot of WASP pilots (from left) Gertrude Meserve, Celia Hunter, Ruth Anderson, and Jo Pitz. The P-47 Thunderbolt behind them was a third heavier than the P-51 Mustang but was also a high-performance World War II aircraft that performed admirably in combat. *Courtesy of WASP Archives, Texas Woman's University Libraries*

The WASPs were furious at what they considered a conspiracy, led by Pearson, who continued to beat the anti-WASP drum in his newspaper columns. He complained, "The government has spent more than $21,000,000 training lady fliers at the behest of vivacious aviatrix Jacqueline Cochran, wife of financial magnate Floyd Odlum. . . . After almost two years of training and the expenditure of millions of dollars, only 11 WASPs are able to fly twin engine pursuit planes and only 3 are qualified to pilot 4 engine bombers."

It was the last statement, especially, that infuriated Gertrude and the other WASPs. She knew the truth—that hundreds of women were performing flight duties across the country every day, sometimes at considerable risk. And they were flying every kind of plane in the US Army's inventory.

Ladies Courageous

Ladies Courageous, starring Loretta Young, was released in 1944. Loosely based on the story of the WASPs, the film was "embarrassing to women pilots, who squirm through seeing it," reported WASP Byrd Howell Granger. A *New York Times* reviewer noted that the film "represents a very curious compliment to the [WASP] . . . and the Army Air Force, which sanctioned and participated in the making of the picture. . . . Such hysterics, such bickering and generally unladylike, nay unpatriotic, conduct on the part of a supposedly representative group of American women this reviewer has never before seen upon the screen."

Gertrude sensed the growing desire of Congress to disband the WASPs and wondered if she had a future in the air. For several days her mind burned with conflict. Marrying Henry would mean giving up the WASPs to take care of a baby. Did she want to be a mother, and at what price? There was also her budding romance with Duncan Miller. He was cute; they had flying in common, and they could talk about aircraft characteristics and handling, weather conditions, and maneuvers for hours.

It was now clear to Gertrude that the war was going to be won by the Allies, but what would she do after it was over?

After sending his initial letter, Vreeland called his daughter, urging her to accept Henry's offer. When her mother

Who Was Drew Pearson?

Andrew Russell "Drew" Pearson (1897–1969) was a popular and powerful muckraking journalist noted for his column Washington Merry-Go-Round, which attacked public figures. In addition to his newspaper column, he had radio programs and appeared in several movies. His one-time partner, Jack Anderson, said Pearson saw journalism as a weapon to be used against those he judged to be working against the public interest. Anderson said that Pearson frequently resorted to combining factual news items with fabricated or unsubstantiated details. His writing attacked both right- and left-wing politicians and causes.

got on the phone, Gertrude felt like all her defenses were scrubbed away, that she was caught in a trap. Reluctantly she called Henry. She agreed to marry him and to raise his niece, Ann. The wedding date was set for September 22, and the ceremony would be held at the Tompkins family farmhouse in Bridgehampton, Long Island.

The night before the wedding, Gertrude sat with her sister Elizabeth. "The atmosphere was heavy with resignation and not happiness," recalled Elizabeth. Gertrude was crying and said she wanted to call the wedding off. Her father and mother entered the room and had a long talk with her, telling her she was just tired and overwrought.

"Obedience was the norm," said Elizabeth. Gertrude loved her father so much she just couldn't let him down. Gertrude understood that the engagement was not to be taken lightly. "She had made a promise, and that was her word," said Laura Whittall-Scherfee, Elizabeth's granddaughter and Gertrude's grandniece.

The next day guests gathered for the wedding ceremony on Long Island. Gertrude and Henry were presented a wedding gift of two adjoining acres in Bridgehampton. Standing in their uniforms, they took their vows before an Episcopal priest. But Elizabeth noticed that Gertrude's thoughts seemed far away, perhaps with her lost first love, Mike Kolendorski.

"I do," Gertrude said. And a moment later she was being kissed by her new husband, Henry Silver.

She was to report back for duty in three days, but in another 60 days she would be through with the WASPs when they disbanded.

After her marriage, Gertrude wrote two letters that mention Henry. One was dated October 18, 1944, and was sent to his older sister, Helen. In this letter she first mentions delivering a P-51 to New York. In a reference to Henry, she wrote, "It won't be long until we are a happily united family." In a letter to Elizabeth dated October 20, 1944, she writes about remaining overnight at the Raleigh-Durham airfield and hitchhiking into town, only to get the last cot available at the YWCA. In this letter she tells Elizabeth that "Henry was very much pleased that you asked him out to B-hampton but he said the

From left: Vreeland Tompkins, Gertrude Tompkins, and Henry Silver on the day of the wedding in Bridgehampton, Long Island. *Photo courtesy of the Whittall family*

transportation from the northern part of [Long Island] is too difficult."

These brief references are all that exist regarding Gertrude's thoughts about Henry Silver after their marriage. Elizabeth was adamant that her sister was unhappy at this time.

14

SEIZED BY THE SUN

A month had passed since the wedding, and on October 26, 1944, Gertrude sat in the cockpit of the new P-51D at Mines Field in Los Angeles as a North American Aviation repairman tinkered with the canopy glide. The repairs would mean a late departure. Other WASPs in her P-51 group had already lifted off and were zooming east.

Gertrude Tompkins was anxious to be in the air.

She looked out at the gauzy orange sun that peered through the haze over the bay. Since now her takeoff was not going to happen until after 3:18 PM, she had been ordered to fly only as far as the air force base in Palm Springs, roughly 100 miles away. She would RON there. The next day she would fly another five hours to Newark, adding to her existing flying time of 350.05 hours.

The mechanic completed his work on the cockpit. Gertrude cranked the handle to bring the Plexiglas canopy forward. Apparently she was satisfied.

"Tower, this is Mustang 669. Request clearance for takeoff."

These were the last words she was ever heard to speak.

She taxied toward the south runway, weaving an S as she'd been taught. She braked. She turned the ship to face into the nearly imperceptible breeze off the ocean. After taking off and looping around, she would soon have the wind behind her as she raced east.

The weather was good, they had told her in the briefing—68 degrees. There was a marine layer this day over Santa Monica Bay. A marine layer is warm air that is cooled by the temperature of the sea, forming a haze. She would climb out of it in seconds. The tower gave her a time check. It was 3:42 PM when Gertrude began rolling, the ringing thunder of the powerful Mustang pulling her toward the misty, orange sun.

It was four days before anyone noticed that Gertrude Tompkins was missing. At Love Field, in Dallas, her base of record, somebody saw she had not filed the required remain-overnight telegram from October 26. With 80 of its women pilots coming and going across the country every day, the Fifth Ferry Group headquarters in Dallas was hard-pressed to keep track of all of them.

A call was placed to the Long Beach WASP coordinating center. Was Gertrude Tompkins still there?

No.

The official was told to call the control tower at Mines Field, where she'd taken off, and see what information they had. There was confusion over the number of the plane she flew. The records said she was in number 662, not 669.

Number 662? Mustang 662 had been delivered, someone noted, but it had been flown by WASP Dorothy Hopkins, not by Gertrude Tompkins.

What about tower clearance? Paperwork problems, came the response. Check Palm Springs and Arizona. Wasn't she supposed to make it to Albuquerque?

She was not in any of the other possible locations.

The war had created an enormous number of flights, and every day was chaotic with aircraft coming and going at what would become Los Angeles International Airport. The common practice for WASPs at the time was to file a flight plan covering all of the day's pilots ferrying P-51s from Mines Field. There were no individual flight plans, so it was impossible to know who left at what time. (One of the changes in procedure after Gertrude's disappearance was that individual flight plans would be filed for each pilot.)

On October 30, 1944, Gertrude Tompkins was declared missing. Clerical oversights and errors resulted in a late start in looking for her. The next morning a search began.

Gertrude Tompkins, 1944.
Courtesy WASP Archive, Texas Woman's University Libraries

15

SEARCHING

It was assumed that Gertrude had flown east. A search of the mountainous area east of Los Angeles began. It concentrated along an area known as Green Airway Five, a flight path that heads east from Los Angeles. Planes from the army air forces and Civil Air Patrol then spread over southern California and western Arizona, but they concentrated their search patterns near Palm Springs, where she had been instructed to stay if she got a late start. The mechanic who fixed her canopy was interviewed and agreed she was headed for Palm Springs.

The day the air force search began, the navy and the coast guard conducted sweeps of Santa Monica Bay and the nearby reaches of the Pacific, but if there were any signs of a crashed airplane, they had been washed away. An oil slick would have dissipated, and there wasn't much on a P-51 that floated.

On November 16, a Civil Air Patrol plane reported possible wreckage near Toro Peak in the Santa Rosa Mountains of Riverside County east of Los Angeles, but what appeared to be wreckage from the air turned out to be a formation of rocks.

Her sister WASPs, flying daily on the route Gertrude was thought to have taken, kept a close eye on the desert and mountain terrain as they flew over it, hoping for a glimpse of reflective aluminum. There was a rumor that one WASP rented a plane and spent hours lingering over the presumed route.

Henry Silver had been notified of Gertrude's disappearance and had shown up in Los Angeles a few days after the search began. The WASPs flying out of Mines Field were surprised to learn their friend Gertrude had been married. She hadn't told any of them. Henry rode along on some search flights and stayed close to the WASP message center in Long Beach. By November 18, three weeks after her disappearance, the search had involved 56 aircraft that had flown 1,067 hours. On that day a halt was called to the search, and Henry was informed of its termination.

On November 22 a representative of the army knocked on the door of Vreeland and Laura Tompkins in Summit, New Jersey. Already informed by Henry of Gertrude's missing plane, Vreeland seated the soldier and escorted his wife from the room. Nearly a month after Gertrude had lifted off the runway in Los Angeles, her father was told that his daughter was officially missing and presumed dead.

Even in grief there were personal items that had to be dealt with. Henry wrote to the air force asking where Gertrude's fur coats had been stored. One was found at Nieman Marcus in Dallas, the other at the Fishburn Oriental Dyeing and Dry

Cleaning Company in Dallas. A total of 204 pounds of personal effects were mailed by the air force to Henry in three separate boxes. Three library books were charged to her account: *Refugees*; *Thomas Jefferson, World Citizen*; and *Mother Russia*. A letter from the law office of Clark, Sickels, and Barton, New York City, was sent on behalf of Henry Silver telling the air force that he was married to Gertrude on September 22, 1944. It inquired how many copies of Gertrude's probated will would be needed by the air force.

A letter was sent from a court officer to Duncan Miller, Gertrude's P-51 pilot friend from Brownsville, reading, "Your letter to WASP Gertrude V. Tompkins was opened and is herewith returned to you," and informing him she had been declared dead.

In a letter to Henry Silver dated January 12, 1945, air force general Hap Arnold told how a plaque had been dedicated on December 7, 1944, to the "memory of those WASP who died while serving their country." He sent Henry a photo of the plaque. He also told him that Henry would shortly receive a Certificate of Service and the Service Pin earned by Gertrude. "I hope you will always feel that you are yourself a member of the Air Forces family."

Questions remained for Henry, for Gertrude's family, and for her friends and fellow WASPs: What happened? Was there a mechanical failure? Or pilot error? One dark possibility was that she flew away from her marriage in the airplane that meant so much to her, expressing her displeasure and despondency over her future in a deliberate crash.

These questions have never been answered. Gertrude Tompkins had almost become a forgotten footnote to the sprawling history of the war. But in 1997 the family's interest was reignited when Ken Whittall-Scherfee, married to Gertrude's grandniece Laura, ran across a book by Pat Macha, an aviation accident historian, titled *Aircraft Wrecks in the Mountains and Deserts of California*. The book was dedicated to Gertrude Tompkins, and one of the entries about a wreck sounded like it could have been about Gertrude.

Macha, a retired Huntington Beach, California, schoolteacher whose father worked in the aviation industry, began his love affair with aircraft at an early age. He became interested in plane crashes in 1963 when he was leading a youth group hike and stumbled across a plane wreck at the 11,000-foot level on San Gorgonio Peak, the highest point in the San Bernardino Mountains. Macha began building a database of crashed aircraft. Since then he has researched and found hundreds of crash sites in California and the West, some dating back to the early 20th century.

Laura and Ken Whittall-Scherfee credit Macha with being the cornerstone of the continued search for Gertrude. After reading Macha's book, said Ken, "We contacted him to find that he was familiar with Gertrude's story. In fact, he said he wondered when someone from her family was going to contact him. He was very interested in helping us try to locate her. Macha had a theory about where the wreck could be found. It made more sense to us than anything we'd heard."

Macha believed the plane's wreckage lay a half mile or less off busy Dockweiler State Beach on Santa Monica Bay. In 1944 Gertrude's takeoff runway ended at Sepulveda Boulevard, about two miles from the beach. Her normal flight path would have been to lift off over the bay and then come left, swinging around from a western heading to an eastern heading.

By 2002 Macha had studied the reports and reasoned that Gertrude might have gotten into trouble on takeoff. Perhaps her balky canopy had come loose, distracting her as she flew in the ocean haze, causing her to take her eyes off her instruments just long enough to become disoriented.

"The 51 is a very hot plane, and you have to stay with it at all times," said Macha. "She was low and moving fast and perhaps the plane smacked into the water, maybe even cartwheeled on impact."

In 1944 Santa Monica Bay was without any housing or commercial development. There were strict wartime laws against straying into sensitive areas, including airports. It was unlikely that anybody was walking the beach that day who would have witnessed a crash, said Macha.

One of the other difficulties was that the wreckage, if in the bay, might be covered by sand, sediment, and sewage. In the years since Gertrude's disappearance, Ballona Creek had carried tons of earth-rich runoff and detritus from the Los Angeles Basin into the sea near Dockweiler. During strong storms it has carried a huge volume—more than 71,000 cubic feet of water per second at times. Hyperion Treatment Plant was another source of sediment. Established in 1894, Hyperion is the oldest sewage treatment plant in Los Angeles. A thick layer of treated sludge had built up in the bay from years of operations at Hyperion.

Laura Whittall-Scherfee wrote a letter to the air force requesting information related to her great-aunt and months later received a package an inch-and-a-half thick containing copies of the military's investigation of Gertrude's disappearance, transcripts of flight training, and more, including a list of items reclaimed from a suitcase and from Gertrude's personal locker at Love Field in Dallas. She gave copies to Macha.

With the family's encouragement, Macha hooked up with Jim Blunt, an ex-police diver. With only rudimentary sonar equipment, Blunt and a team of family, friends, and volunteers from the San Bernardino Coroner's office (who had helped Macha in the past) boarded a boat and scanned an area three miles long and a mile wide off the end of LAX's runways. A dozen dives over several days turned up nothing in the murky water.

Meanwhile, Laura contacted Huntington Beach congressional representative Dana Rohrabacher to get the military involved. The navy wrote Laura saying a search would cost too much, $2 million in taxpayers' money. The responding admiral said that any wreckage older than 50 years falls under the jurisdiction of the National Historic Preservation Act, which would pose potential legal barriers to doing anything with the wreckage even if it were found.

Undeterred, the Whittall-Scherfees, Macha, Blunt, and volunteers returned to the site. Using a sophisticated magnetometer capable of locating certain metals buried on the ocean bottom, in five days they turned up 300 toilets that enterprising fishermen had dumped into the ocean as hotels for lobsters. The next summer they were back, this time with more powerful sonar equipment.

Hopes rose when they saw a series of unusual lines on the sounding recorder, a device that inks a profile of the seafloor. They were in about 18 feet of water. To Jim Blunt, it was definitely the profile of an airplane. "It is metal, all right." He and other divers poked probes at least four feet into the seafloor and turned up nothing. Coming to the surface, Blunt estimated that the plane, if there was one, was under 15 or 20 feet of sediment and sand. The water was so algae-loaded and warm that the group now waited for colder weather, when the clarity of the water would improve.

They conducted more searches and succeeded in eliminating some possibilities. But as the searching continued, Macha and the Whittall-Scherfees found no wreckage that would indicate it was Gertrude's P-51D.

In 1999 Gary Fabian, another Huntington Beach resident, had become fascinated by seafloor research conducted by the US Geological Survey (USGS). As a recreational fisherman, he knew that structures on the ocean floor attracted fish. And the USGS had perfected a technology for finding such structures. It was called multibeam sonar (MBS), and it was being used to map the coastal waters around America. The shapes of sunken ships and airplanes stand out vividly on many of the USGS images.

Using MBS, in 2001 Fabian and his partner Ray Arntz made a major discovery in Santa Monica Bay: the UB88, the only German submarine ever sunk off the Pacific Coast. It was considered the most elusive shipwreck in California waters. A World War I trophy, it had been used as target practice and sunk by the US Navy in 1921.

On August 19, 2003, at his home in Huntington Beach, Gary Fabian read a story about Macha finding a World War II navy torpedo bomber in the water off San Diego. Fabian contacted Macha immediately. In 2005 the combined

Fabian-Macha team renewed the search for Gertrude's P-51 in Santa Monica Bay. In the meantime, Macha had found a man he believed was an eyewitness to the crash of Gertrude's P-51.

The eyewitness was Frank Jacobs, a retired aerospace engineer from Redondo Beach, California. Jacobs had read a newspaper account of Macha's search for Gertrude and notified him that in the month of October 1944, when he was 12 years old, he was fishing off the Manhattan Beach Pier. The pier is 3.8 miles south of the western end of the runway from which Gertrude lifted off.

He said he had just arrived at the pier on a cloudy day when a loud engine noise prompted him to look north. He watched a fighter plane climb after taking off from the airport's southern runway. Suddenly there was a sharp drop in the noise level and the plane's engine began sputtering. He said the plane angled over into a shallow dive that became steeper before it disappeared in the fog bank hanging offshore.

Jacobs remembers two nearby adults saying something about a P-51 Mustang.

"This event left a very strong, vivid impression on me as a 12-year-old boy," Jacobs said. "I sensed that someone must have died." He said he was surprised when nothing appeared in the next day's papers.

"It was definitely that year, that month," insisted Jacobs.

Macha is certain that Jacobs saw Gertrude's plane go down. He'd been looking for an eyewitness and he finally had one. The Fabian-Macha team met Jacobs on the pier, and he pointed to where he had seen the plane falter.

"We took a heading on it and began to search," said Macha. "We were crossing targets off our list when we thought we'd found her plane. It turned out we had found a T-33 Shooting

Star jet trainer, missing since 1950 with two men aboard." They found no trace of Gertrude's P-51.

Undaunted, in 2009 they began the most ambitious and thorough search they had yet undertaken in the quest for Gertrude's plane. Fabian flew in from Texas, joining Pat Macha and a group called the Missing Aircraft Search Team. Fabian had identified more than 70 targets they would investigate. Divers came from as far away as the East Coast. During an intensive week they found lots of junk, including more toilets, small boats, a washer and dryer, and piles of rock, probably dropped by barges carrying them from quarries on Catalina Island.

The most exciting find was a missing Cessna 210, previously unlocated. But there was not a hint of Gertrude Tompkins's P-51. The search continues even today, and the mystery remains unsolved. It is possible that Gertrude and her plane will be lost to history.

Macha is sure it's in Santa Monica Bay. Fabian is not so sure.

"We've scoured the bay. It's possible we missed her; I don't rule that out. But we really focused on the areas just off the runways and it just wasn't there," said Fabian. "Maybe she flew farther off-shore before she crashed."

Macha thinks this is unlikely, saying WASPs did not like flying over the ocean. They were not trained for it. When taking off from Los Angeles, they invariably made a sweeping left turn and headed inland. He believes Jacobs's account of seeing the plane falter and thinks it plummeted into the bay, perhaps now covered with material from the sewage treatment plant or from outflow from Ballona Creek.

"It's fascinated all of us," said Fabian. "But it's possible that she's up in the mountains or out in the desert."

A kind of cult of searchers and interested followers has grown up around the woman whose stutter disappeared forever when she raced into the blue on silver wings. The passion of her family and aircraft historians ensures that the search will continue into the foreseeable future.

EPILOGUE

It became a family tradition to call out "Be sure and look for Gertrude!" whenever her relatives set off on travels. At the time of her disappearance, both sisters, Elizabeth Tompkins Whittall and Margaret Tompkins Wade, considered the possibility that Gertrude had flown off and into hiding. She was unhappy with her marriage, and her career as a WASP was coming to an end. Was it possible that she flew to Mexico, ditched her plane, and started life with a new identity? Entertaining this notion was one way the family dealt with the heartbreak of this unsolved mystery, a tragedy that two generations of Gertrude's survivors have lived with.

For Ken and Laura Whittall-Scherfee the search for Laura's great-aunt Gertrude had become part of the fabric of their lives, ever since Laura sent her first letter to the air force. The family needed some kind of closure, but search after search had revealed no hint of what had happened to Gertrude's P-51.

At a WASP reunion in 2002, 200 WASPs and their guests sat at tables in a US Air Force hanger at Davis-Monthan Air Force Base near Tucson, Arizona. WASP numbers were dwindling as age claimed the valiant fliers.

Among the guests were Ken and Laura. They moved among the crowd, talking with WASPs who had known Gertrude, gleaning information from the misty memories of women who piloted World War II's airplanes. They sat with Mickey Axton, who wanted to know all about what they had learned during the latest search. Mickey was Gertrude's closest friend in the WASPs and flew with her at Pecos. Mickey believed that she, too, had been ferrying a plane out of Los Angeles the same day as Gertrude's last flight.

The WASPs in attendance were mostly in their vigorous eighties and even nineties, hair neatly set and curled in shades of white and gray and pale blue.

They had volunteered to fly at a time when their country was fighting for its survival, during the darkest days early in World War II, when America was desperate for pilots. During the brief lifespan of the WASPs the women had flown over 60 million miles in service to their country.

This night they called out to old friends, squinting at name tags, talking in groups of four and five, sometimes hugging, sometimes holding hands. Many still flew, and some had piloted their own planes to the semiannual convention. Several used canes or walkers. Some still fit into their uniforms, and many wore their silver WASP pilot wings.

They looked on, bright-eyed and expectant, as they waited for the honor guard to begin the evening with the presentation of colors. Proud women unafraid of displays of patriotism, they fidgeted and looked for Old Glory. Where were the colors? There were mutterings amid the tinkle of glasses.

"I can't forget that there were 25,000 applicants for my job," said former WASP Vivian Eddy, peering over stylish half-glasses, as she waited.

"Do you remember Margie Collins? Couldn't do lazy eights and so they washed her out. She was heartbroken."

"The Chinese girl who died in the P-40 in Great Falls—what was her name?"

"Hazel Ying Lee."

Heads nodded, remembering.

"Burned in her cockpit after a horrible crash." Silence, as if to honor the dead.

Ten minutes passed. The young air force officers at the head table, hosts for this reunion, muttered nervously, sipping their drinks. One of the officers busily punched at her cell phone. Food servers lounged in clumps of three and four, waiting for the signal to start.

The honor guard and the American flag were still glaringly absent.

The air force major with the cell phone finally rose and took the microphone, her features flushed.

"I'm sorry ladies. There's been a foul-up. The honor guard will not be with us tonight."

"Well, what did you expect?" said one of the ladies in the audience loudly. "We're WASPs. We've always been overlooked." Ironic laughter rippled through the crowd, but the truth was discrimination was something the women never got used to. Once again the WASPs had received the back of their government's hand, an attitude that lingered as a vestige of a war that ended 57 years before.

But they were no longer resigned to the discrimination and injustice that went with being a female pilot, a fly girl, as they'd been called during the war. The old feelings surfaced at the tables in the hanger. They were tired of hearing that the WASPs were "nothing but glamour girls in pretty uniforms." They were angry at being marginalized.

Thirty-eight WASPS died in the line of duty flying for their country. Why couldn't they be buried in Arlington National Cemetery, where other veterans had the right to be laid to rest?

The WASPs were never paid the same as regular air force pilots. They were never granted rank or military status, insurance or hospitalization. Their requests for veteran's benefits were brushed aside.

Their premature and poorly managed dismissal from service in late 1944, a sad chapter in America's military history, resided painfully in the heart of every WASP at the banquet that evening.

As the salad was placed before her, WASP Mickey Axton brought up Gertrude Tompkins Silver. Some of them remembered Gertrude, how she never seemed to quite fit in.

"Perhaps it was because she was older," a woman with white hair said, and suddenly the focus of the table was this mysterious and handsome woman who took off in her P-51 that day, never to be seen again.

Before her death, Mickey Axton said, "We need to find Gertrude. We need all members accounted for. Because all we have now is a sky full of memories."

★ ★ ★

AFTERWORD

was researching another writing project in 1999 when I came across the story of Gertrude Tompkins Silver. Digging into her story, I grew to like and admire a woman who has been presumed dead since 1944. She haunts every page of this book.

Hers is the amazing story of a woman overcoming a lifelong handicap during a few magical minutes in the sky. It is also a uniquely American story, resonating with our desire for fair play and our cheers for the underdog. We want Gertrude's stutter to be cured, and we also want the WASPs to be recognized and honored for their unique contribution. These intrepid fliers were overlooked and discriminated against for too many years, yet there is no question that they changed America's attitude about women pilots.

Gertrude's sister, Elizabeth Tompkins Whittall, lived in Vero Beach, Florida. When I began my interviews and correspondence with her in 2002 she was 93. In conversations and subsequent correspondence, she proved to be full of life and very open about the family history. Her memoir, *From There to Here*, provides many insights into her family and into Gertrude's life. Elizabeth died in 2010 at 101.

My interviews with Elizabeth and with Ken and Laura Whittall-Scherfee were the basis for this book. Ken and Laura live in California, and it was my pleasure to spend time with them recording their memories, the family history, and the speculation as to what may have happened to Gertrude. Over the years we exchanged frequent communication by phone and mail. They read this manuscript for accuracy in 2015, as did some of Laura's family, all relatives of Gertrude.

Henry Silver, Gertrude's widower husband and Vreeland Tompkins's "second son," succeeded Vreeland as president of Smooth-On Inc. in 1950 and continued in that capacity until his death in 1964, at age 61. Henry never remarried, and his daughter, Ann Vreeland Wood, says he mourned Gertrude until the day he died.

Ann Vreeland Wood never met her stepmother. Henry adopted her as a baby, and she was raised by him in the MacDougal Street apartments until his death. She dropped the Silver from her name and goes by Ann Vreeland Wood.

Ann said there were "so many stories, including one that Gertrude was on her way home to take care of me when she crashed." She said many of them were designed to protect her from the knowledge of the circumstances surrounding her birth. Ann lives in New Mexico with her husband. She's an avid birdwatcher.

Vreeland Tompkins, Gertrude's father, died in 1957, and her mother, Laura, lived to be 91 and died in 1977. Gertrude's sister Margaret Tompkins Wade died in 1976.

I was fortunate to have begun this project when some of the original WASPs were still attending reunions and staying in communication with one another. As I interviewed them, they referred me to others who knew Gertrude Tompkins, creating a network of informants.

I interviewed Duncan Miller, Gertrude's fellow pilot in Brownsville, by telephone at his home in Vacaville, California, where he owned six planes, including a fully restored BT-13 Vibrator, one of the planes Gertrude flew and disliked during basic training.

Many of the tales of Gertrude's life as a WASP came from women who flew with her or knew her while in the WASPs, including Mickey Axton and Winifred Wood. Their interviews were a delight, casting light on a unique period when women reached for the sky. After the WASP era, it would be several decades before women pilots would once again be in cockpits and at the controls in a military setting. Mickey Axton lived in Arizona and died in 2010. Win Wood lived near Palm Springs and died in 2009.

Gertrude's WASP training, service, and search are also supported by military documents.

Fewer than 100 WASPs are still living at the time of this writing, but the memories of those who have passed are kept alive by their children, grandchildren, and by institutions dedicated to WASP history. The WASPs were finally recognized by Congress in 1977 and were granted benefits similar to those of other World War II veterans. In 2002 the first WASP was allowed interment in Arlington National Cemetery, although in 2015 these privileges were withdrawn by the secretary of the army. After pressure from families of WASPs as well as current female military pilots, WASP Elaine D. Harmon was allowed burial in Arlington on September 5, 2016.

In 2010 Laura Whittall-Scherfee was the recipient of the Congressional Gold Medal on behalf of Gertrude. This gathering of several hundred family members and WASPs provided long-overdue recognition to the WASPs for their service during World War II. The two-day event began with a memorial service for the 38 WASPs who died in service to their country. A family member for each of the missing sat on the front row. One by one as each name was read aloud, a family representative placed a red rose on a pedestal. Laura Whittall-Scherfee was proud to be the family representative for Gertrude. "It was an experience I will never forget," she said. The memorial service occurred at the Air Force Memorial in Arlington, Virginia, and culminated with the air force "missing man" formation flying overhead. The Congressional Gold Medal was awarded the next day in a ceremony in the Rotunda of the US Capitol.

On December 3, 2015, the US secretary of defense, Ash Carter, for the first time authorized American women for combat. It was recognition that the thousands of women who served in Iraq and Afghanistan—many of whom were killed or wounded—were in combat whether designated for it or not.

Regarding Stanley Michael "Mike" Kolendorski, Gertrude's first love: Originally from New Jersey, he was an American pilot who flew for the Royal Air Force. He fought the Germans in England's Eagle Squadron 71 before America got into the war. During the war, 244 Americans flew in RAF Eagle Squadrons, and 71 were killed. I tried to learn more about him from the Royal Air Force but was told that only family members could have access to pilots' casualty information. Eventually I found Mike's surviving nephew living in New Jersey. He had never met his late uncle but had been named for him. He graciously contacted the RAF and was able to get confirmation of Pilot Officer Kolendorski's death. He conveyed to me the information used in this book.

Elizabeth Whittall was not certain this was the man her sister had loved. I reviewed the information from the RAF records with her, and she thought it sounded right, but . . . She had heard the man's name, but by the time I asked her to recall it she could only say she thought "it started with a C." More than 75 years later, we can never be absolutely certain who Gertrude's first love was, but Kolendorski is the likeliest candidate to fit the information and the time frame. He was born in New Jersey, left on a motorcycle for California during the Depression, and had married and divorced in California before joining the RAF. I am grateful to his namesake and nephew, Stanley Michael Kolendorski, for accessing the RAF files as a next of kin and sharing them with me.

ACKNOWLEDGMENTS

To all the Tompkins family members, friends, and acquaintances of Gertrude's whose assistance I described in the afterword, I extend my sincere and heartfelt thanks.

Additionally, I appreciate Pat Macha for his time in filling me in on his search efforts and technology. He also provided much information about how aircraft were utilized in World War II. Jim Blunt told me about diving for the wreck. I am also indebted to Gary Fabian, who with Pat Macha has spent many hours in researching and hunting for Gertrude's P-51.

I spent countless hours with the late Bob Ivory in his Cessna 172 flying across the West. He was a wonderful instructor. Two other former military pilots and personal friends, Lou Siegel and Kevin McCarthy, provided information that enabled me to add color and dimension to this narrative.

I cannot overlook the hard work of my agents, Sheree Bykofsky and her colleague Janet Rosen. They encouraged me and helped shape the proposal that resulted in this work. Lisa Reardon at Chicago Review Press improved this book with her careful editing and thoughtful suggestions. Claudia Wood worked very hard to make sure *Seized by the Sun* was accurate in every detail. Ellen Hornor meticulously shepherded the book through the production process, and Sarah Olson gets high praise for her jacket design and interior layout.

I am indebted to Lavina Fielding Anderson, who read this manuscript in its youth and made important suggestions. She has been a friend and an astute reader for 20 years.

Thank you to all the others who helped with Gertrude's story: Judith F. Duchan, emeritus professor from the Department of Communicative Disorders and Sciences at the University of Buffalo; Margaret Hatch, PhD, psychologist, Salt Lake City, Utah; the US Air Force Records Division; the US Army Records Division; the Royal Air Force Personnel Management Agency (Casualty); Winifred Wood, WASP 43-W-7; Mickey Axton, WASP 43-W-7; Betty Blake, WASP 43-W-1; Lela Lowder Harding, WASP 43-W-7; Kimberly Johnson, director, Special Collections and University Archivist, Woman's Collection, WASP Archives, Texas Women's University Libraries, Denton; Dawn Letson, Official Archives, Women's Air Force Service, Texas Women's University; Corynthia Dorgan, Official Archives, Texas Women's University Libraries, Denton; Sarah Swan, Public Affairs Division, National Museum of the US Air Force; Nancy Parrish of Wings Across America; the children and grandchildren of WASPs and others who are active with the WASP user group on Yahoo, especially Andy

Hailey, Amy Nathan, Chig Lewis, and Katherine Sharp Land-deck. Their exchanges kept me apace of the WASP network.

I know I have overlooked some who helped during the course of writing this book, and I want to thank them and offer apologies.

I hope that someday Gertrude is found.

As Virginia Allison wrote, "For my soul lies dormant, restless, waiting for that moment when shackles are cast aside and it is free to fly once more."

US AIR FORCE LIST OF GERTRUDE TOMPKINS SILVER'S PERSONAL EFFECTS RECOVERED FROM FOOTLOCKERS AND QUARTERS

B elow is a reproduction of the official air force inventory from undated and unsigned typed sheets. The inventory was probably compiled from lockers at the different bases from which Gertrude flew. All spelling and punctuation are from the original documents. The checks are from friends and relatives and were probably birthday gifts. Gertrude went missing before receiving them.

(Page 1)

3 Lipsticks
4 Spools Thread
2 Negative prints of photo
1 Razor container, empty
11 Panties, silk

1 Cloth bag full of silk hose
1 Garter belt
1 Slip, silk
2 Brassieres
2 Girdles

(Page 1 continued)

1 Hat, black
2 Pr. Gloves, pigskin, white
6 Handkerchiefs
Green material for curtains
1 Basket containing:
    3 Necklaces, beaded
    3 Pr. Earrings
    1 Clip (Costume jewelry)
1 Pr. Wings, WASP
1 Small lapel wings insignia
1 Bunch Artificial Flowers
2 Neckties
4 Pr. Socks
1 Washcloth
1 Cosmetic pouch
1 Cap
2 Kerchiefs
1 Tobacco pouch
1 Pr. Silk stockings
1 Small leather photo fold
3 Hair nets
2 Belts
1 Ball wool mending thread
1 Kodak slide
1 Wooden trinket
1 Shoe cloth
1 Small clock in carrying case
1 Small alarm clock (Baby Ben)
1 Booklet of needles
1 Card of knitting needles
1 Ring box, empty

1 Pencil sharpener (Don. Duck)
1 Napkin, blue
1 Shoehorn
1 Radio, Emerson, portable
1 Compact
1 Photo
1 Book, PAAF Personnel
1 Book, 5th FG Love Field
  Personnel
1 Purse, leather, black, initials
  GVT, containing
    1 small change purse with
     $.50
    1 Bond application
    1 Penny
    1 Handkerchief
    1 Box Eversharp lead
    1 Pack Midol tablets
    3 Leather name bands
    2 Wooden pencils
1 Purse, white, zipper,
  containing:
    1 Change purse
    2 Wooden pencils
    1 Small brass plate bear-
     ing inscription Bev S
1 Dead Reckoning Computer
  and case
1 Pilot's log book
1 Notebook
3 Photographs

1 Leather purse containing:
    1 1000 Reis Brazilian
      coin
    1 Coral Bagles (sic) car
      token
    1 Netherland 5¢ coin
    1 6¢ air mail stamp
1 Computer
2 Books, "Sex Habits" and
  "The Sex Technique in
  Marriage".
1 Silk scarf, white
4 Slips
3 Neckties

1 Bathrobe
3 Dresses, 2-black, 1-purple,
  1-pastel multi-colored
1 Wash cloth
1 Shirt, rayon
1 Housecoat, rayon
3 Pr. Heavy wool socks, white
1 Belt, blue
1 Large straw hat
1 Button, green
1 Pr. shoes, low black
The above items will be found
  in the trunk (footlocker).

(Page 2)

1 Pr. Silk Stockings
1 Sm. alarm clock, portable
  (case)
1 Belt, cloth, black
1 Tin can, round, containing:
    1 checkbook on Rep. Nat.
      Bk. of Dallas
    1 Necktie
    1 Tobacco pouch
    1 Sm. Brass plate initials
      MLD
    1 Identification tape
    1 Sewing kit
    1 Lapel wings insignia
    1 Measuring tape

    3 Spools thread, brown
    1 Thimble
    1 Pr. small scissors
    1 Ribbon, purple, ½"
    3 A. C. Insignias
    1 Pr. Breast wings
    2 ATC Insignia
    79 Pennies (white) in blue
      pack
    1 Under jersey
    1 Under drawers
1 Cosmetic carrying case,
  leather, zipper
1 Can tennis balls (Duncan)
11 Photographs

2 Pilot's log books
1 Pr. high leather boots
7 Brassiers
5 Balls of yarn, khaki
1 Towel, bath
1 Kerchief
1 Wool sweater, white
1 Laundry bag
1 Pr. slippers
1 Pr. leather gloves
1 Small haircomb
1 card bobby pins
1 Leather carrying case (shoulder strap)
1 Small nail file case
1 Hair comb
2 Hair brushes
2 Silk panties
2 Night gowns, flannel (pink, blue)
1 Cotton panties
1 Pr. white gloves
6 handkerchiefs
2 Silk slips
1 Blouse, blue
1 Sweater, button
1 Bathing suit
1 Bag, straw
1 Pr. moccasin
1 Pr. Bedroom slippers, blue
1 Pr. green shoes
1 Pr. black shoes (in mittens)

1 Pr. shoes, black
1 Pr. white gloves
1 Leather bag, zipper, containing lotions, creams, perfumes, etc.
1 Raincoat
1 Leather belt
1 Coat, black, with pilot's wings'
2 Blouse, white
3 Slips
1 Skirt, multi-colored
2 Dresses, multi-colored
1 Skirt, blue
1 Blouse, green
1 Dress, black & White stripes with red belt
1 Dress, upper white, lower multi-colored
1 Dress, green, with belt
1 Trousers, riding, khaki
1 Brassiere
1 Canvas carrying bag with zipper
1 Argus model C2 camera with case
1 Weston light indicator for camera case
1 Kodak film
1 Argus yellow filter lens accessory for camera
1 Coverall, WASP Flying Suit
1 Raincoat with cap

1 Housecoat

1 Necktie

1 Book, "The Apostle"

1 Photograph frame

1 small luggage bag with snaps

1 Pr. socks, wool, white

1 shoe brush

8 Books

1 Straw weave suitcase containing Costume jewelry,
Mexican hats

1 Book o Psalms

1 Prayer Book for Soldiers and
Sailors

4 Photos

2 Books

1 Pr. wool socks

2 Handkerchiefs

1 Air rifle, pump

1 Umbrella, lady's

1 Lady's purse, black

2 Shirts, green

1 Pr. trousers, green

(Second letter of air force inventory, undated)

1 Certificate of Complete of WASP Training Courses

1 Diploma from 568th AAFBU, 4th OUT, Brownsville, Texas

November and December bank statement from Republic
National Bank, Dallas, Texas

1 Letter from Chief of Police, Summit, New Jersey

1 Letter from Phoenix Mutual Life Insurance Company

1 Series E War Bond, $25.00 denomination, in gift folder

1 Series E War Bond, $50.00 denomination, p.o.d. Miss Margaret
P Whittall

1 Letter from H. D. Tompkins containing a check dated 26 Oct.,
1944, in amount of $75.00 drawn by Harold D. Tompkins pay-
able to the order of Gertrude V. Tompkins

1 Letter from Harriet J. Wade containing Cashiers Check NO.
T-7277, dated 19 Oct., 1944, on the Central Hanover Bank and

Trust Co., New York, in amount of $15.00, payable to the order of Gertrude V. Tompkins

1 Letter from Suzanne Van Dulun containing check dated 21 Oct., 1944, in amount of $10.00, payable to the order of Gertrude V. Tompkins.

7 Letters from various persons
4 Letters from H. M. Silver
1 War Department Form No. 58; 1 Treasury Department Form W-2; 1 Class A Pay Reservation.
1 Flying V, 29 September, 1944 issue
1 Clipping containing picture of 3 WASPs, including Gertrude V. Tompkins
2 Keys, one of which is to the footlocker which has been previously shipped.
$1.15 in cash

GENERAL BARTON YOUNT'S TRIBUTE TO WASPs KILLED IN SERVICE

O n December 7, 1944, at the last graduation of WASPs, General Barton K. Yount, commanding general of the army air forces training command, recognized the women who were killed while flying for their country.

Let us acknowledge the measure of their sacrifice by honoring them as brave women, and by honoring them as women who served without thought of glory which we accord to heroes of battle. The service pilot faces the risk of death without the emotional inspiration of combat. Men who battle in the sky have the grim, triumphant knowledge that their bombs and bullets are destroying the enemy, and their courage is sustained by the emotions of conflict.

These women have given their lives in the performance of arduous and exacting duties without being able to see and feel the final results of their work under the quickening influence of aerial action. They have demonstrated a courage which is sustained not by the fevers of combat, but the steady heartbeat of faith—a faith in the rightness of our cause, and a faith in the importance of their work to the men who do go into combat.

Let us pay tribute to these women by honoring their memory. . . . Let us treasure their memory as women whose sacrifice has brought honor not only to their country, but also to their organization.

We shall not forget the accomplishments of our women fliers and their contributions to the fulfillment of our mission. And we shall always keep and remember the brave heritage of the women who gave their lives. It is the heritage of faith in victory and faith in the ultimate freedom of humanity.

NOTES

PROLOGUE: LOST WINGS

in spite of a haze: Jim Radcliff, untitled article, *South Bay Daily Breeze,* September 2, 1997.

It was brand new, one of 45 Mustangs: Brig. Gen. Bob E. Nowland, US Army Air Force, letter marked CONFIDENTIAL to Commanding General, Air Transport Command, 31 October 1944, author's collection.

As a former test pilot, Gertrude, or Tommy: Federal Aviation Administration, *Policies and Regulations,* 1995, Preflight checklist for pilots (formalized by FAA in the 1930s, exact date unknown).

Gertrude placed her small leather flight bag: Granger, *On Final Approach: The Women Air Force Service Pilots of World War II,* 27.

She knew how this plane would perform: US Army Air Force, First Motion Picture Unit, *Flight Characteristics of the P-51 Airplane,* 1944, www.zenoswarbirdvideos.com.

Factory-new airplanes often experienced problems: Pat Macha, interview by author, 2003.

Since she was going to get a late start: US Army Air Force, Report of Major Accident, Form 14, October 26, 1944.

1: IT'S AWFUL HAVING A STUTTER

She came from a wealthy family: Whittall, *From There to Here*, 9.

The Vreeland farm: Robert F. Tompkins and Claire F. Tompkins, "The Tompkins Genealogy," undated document.

"She was very strong minded": Elizabeth Tompkins Whittall, telephone interview by author, November 20, 2002.

They married on May 18, 1904: Whittall, *From There to Here*, 16.

Their first child, Stuart, died at birth: Tompkins Whittall, telephone interview by author, November 20, 2002.

By age four: Whittall, *From There to Here*, 19.

Friends and family volunteered explanations: Tompkins Whittall, telephone interview by author, November 20, 2002.

"The child was frightened as a baby": Elizabeth Tompkins Whittall, telephone interview by author, January 4, 2003. See also Judith Maginnis Kuster, "Folk Myths About Stuttering," The Stuttering Home Page, Department of Speech, Hearing and Rehabilitation Services, Minnesota State University, Mankato, last updated November 14, 2014, www.mnsu.edu /comdis/kuster/Infostuttering/folkmyths.html.

Vreeland took a special interest: Whittall, *From There to Here*, 18–20.

"S-s-someone else always said": Tompkins Whittall, telephone interview by author, January 4, 2003.

The definition of stuttering: The Stuttering Foundation website, www.stutteringhelp.org.

The doctor put Gertrude through: Tompkins Whittall, telephone interview by author, January 4, 2003. See also Judith Duchan,

"History of Speech-Pathology," State University of New York at Buffalo, May 12, 2011, www.acsu.buffalo.edu/~duchan /new_history/overview.html.

"If we do this every time": Tompkins Whittall, telephone interview by author, January 4, 2003.

She became close to the household's: Whittall, *From There to Here*, 2.

"this dear, sweet" African American couple": Whittall, *From There to Here*, 2.

Christmas brought excitement: Whittall, *From There to Here*, 13.

Gertrude sang, "Things are seldom": Tompkins Whittall, telephone interview by author, January 4, 2003. The song is from the comic opera *H.M.S. Pinafore* by Gilbert and Sullivan.

The family continued to search: Tompkins Whittall, telephone interview, November 20, 2002.

2: CHILDHOOD UPS AND DOWNS

Jersey City is home to: Whittall, *From There to Here*, 3.

"so it was wise": Whittall, *From There to Here*, 4.

"The mile walk to school": Whittall, *From There to Here*, 4.

"My n-n-n-name is Little Gertrude": Elizabeth Tompkins Whittall, telephone interview by author, October 2002 and January 4, 2003. See also Vicki Benson Schutter, "For Richer, Poorer, or Fluenter," April 7, 1997, www.mnsu.edu/comdis/kuster /PWSspeak/schutter2.html.

"Our whole family revolved": Whittall, *From There to Here*, 8.

Rosaline was said to be: Whittall, *From There to Here*, 10.

Entertainment, 1920s Style: Digital History website, www.digital history.uh.edu/disp_textbook.cfm?smtID=2&psid=3397.

severe headaches: Whittall, *From There to Here*, 15.

While visiting Laura one weekend: Whittall, *From There to Here*, 23.

"How blessed we were": Whittall, *From There to Here*, 24.

"We catched fish and talked": Tompkins Whittall, telephone interview with author, January 4, 2003. Elizabeth said her sister loved reading Mark Twain, especially *Huckleberry Finn.*

In 1926 Grandmother Rosaline died: Whittall, *From There to Here,* 10; Tompkins Whittall, telephone interviews with author, October 2002 and January 4, 2003.

Elizabeth, who was said to have a "way" with hair: Whittall, *From There to Here,* 10.

"When I reached the appropriate": Whittall, *From There to Here,* 17.

She felt shamed by her inability: Whittall, *From There to Here,* 20.

3: CONFIDENCE GROWS

Spring brought a flush: Tompkins Whittall, telephone interviews by author, October 2002 and January 4, 2003.

"Give her enough books": Tompkins Whittall, telephone interviews by author, October 2002 and January 4, 2003.

"It was a disaster": Whittall, *From There to Here,* 54; Elizabeth Tompkins Whittall, interview by author, 2003.

In the spring: Ronald L. Heinemann, "The Great Depression in Virginia," *Encyclopedia Virginia,* September 14, 2012, www.encyclopediavirginia.org/great_depression_in_virginia.

"And you want to be a farmer?": Tompkins Whittall, telephone interviews by author, October 2002 and January 4, 2003.

Gertrude arrived on the Ambler campus: Tompkins Whittall, telephone interview by author, January 4, 2003.

The Pennsylvania School of Horticulture for Women: "Pennsylvania School of Horticulture for Women Historical Marker," ExplorePAHistory.com, 2011, http://explorepahistory.com/hmarker.php?markerId=1-A-130.

The Great Depression was spreading: Manchester, *The Glory and the Dream: A Narrative History of America, 1932–1972,* 35–82.

"Yes," he said, "it was called the Dark Ages": Manchester, *Glory and the Dream*, 35.

"terrible all over" and all quotes through "I made a compost pile": Gertrude Tompkins, letter to Elizabeth Tompkins Whittall, 26 October 1930; Elizabeth Tompkins Whittall, telephone interviews by author, 2002 and 2003.

However, there were still many rich people in America: History Detectives, PBS, season 7, episode 7, August 10, 2009.

The Depression and Music: "The Music Industry," The Great Depression—A Dupuis Web Quest, http://dupuisdepression .weebly.com/music.html; Kelly Mitchell, "Swing Music," *Music During the Great Depression* (blog), http://musicduring thegreatdepression.blogspot.com/p/swing-music-of-great -depression-kelly.html.

Vreeland's Smooth-On Business: Tompkins Whittall, interview by author, January 4, 2003. Predictions of replacement of cast iron were made as early as February 8, 1888, in the *American Engineer*, 50. Cast iron still finds some application in industry, as well as in cookware.

After Ambler, Gertrude made: Tompkins Whittall, interview by author, January 4, 2003; Heinemann, "The Great Depression in Virginia."

Politically, Gertrude found herself: Tompkins Whittall, interview by author, January 4, 2003.

In spite of President Herbert Hoover: Manchester, *Glory and the Dream*, 83.

"Take a method and try it": Franklin D. Roosevelt, speech to Oglethorpe University, May 22, 1932, http://newdeal.feri .org/speeches/1932d.htm.

"One Roosevelt was one too many": Tompkins Whittall, telephone interview by author, January 4, 2003.

4: TRAVELING ABROAD

For young women of wealth: Gertrude's travels through Europe are from memories of Tompkins Whittall, interview by author, January 4, 2003.

5: FINDING HER FOOTING

True to her dream, she bought two Saanens: Whittall, *From There to Here*, 20.

"Goats as a Hobby": New Zealand information is contained in an undated newspaper clipping in possession of Elizabeth Whittall's granddaughter, Laura Whittall-Scherfee.

In 1936 polio struck Elizabeth: Whittall, *From There to Here*, 75.

She still considered goats her passion: Gertrude's move to NYC was described by her sister Elizabeth Tompkins Whittall, interview by author, January 4, 2003.

To help her father, and to "keep the money in the family": Tompkins Whittall, interviews by author, 2002 and 2003.

Why Gertrude Loved Goats: Cleon V. Kimberling, "Introductory Information on Pet Goats," Goat World, www.goatworld.com/articles/goatsaspets/petgoats.shtml.

Gertrude went apartment hunting: Manhattan telephone directory, 1939.

The owner of her building, a Yale graduate: Ann Vreeland Wood, adopted daughter of Henry Silver, interview by author, January 15, 2003.

"Deceit is a place to sit down": Elizabeth Tompkins Whittall, interview by author, January 6, 2003.

Henry wooed her ardently: Tompkins Whittall, interview by author, January 6, 2003.

6: TAKING FLIGHT

Reading the pages of the New York Times: "Historical Events in 1940," On This Day, www.historyorb.com/events/date/1940.

While America was struggling: Gilbert, *A History of the Twentieth Century,* 159–259.

Japan's government was under: Manchester, *Glory and the Dream,* 150.

In the 1930s a majority of Americans: Manchester, *Glory and the Dream,* 207.

Some American pilots: Merryman, *Clipped Wings: The Rise and Fall of the Women Airforce Service Pilots (WASPs) of World War II,* 10.

President Franklin D. Roosevelt convened: Manchester, *Glory and the Dream,* 290.

It was probably at a dance: Elizabeth Tompkins Whittall letter to grandson Paul Whittall, 2010.

her sister's "one and only" love: Tompkins Whittall, interview by author, January 4, 2003.

Gertrude's first flight must have been: Cole, *Women Pilots of World War II,* 7.

"My first flight was a stunning": Cole, *Women Pilots,* 8.

In May 1941: Stan Kolendorski, nephew of Stanley Michael Kolendorski, letter to author, 11 February 2003.

Some women pilots got their licenses: Merryman, *Clipped Wings,* 11.

In 1941, about 3,000 American women: Granger, *On Final Approach,* 6.

7: THE WASPS ARE BORN

There were many reasons women: Cole, *Women Pilots,* 7.

"For each of us": Cole, *Women Pilots,* 7.

Like Gertrude, WASP Nadine Nagle's: Merryman, *Clipped Wings,* 15.

"In the summer of 1942": Merryman, *Clipped Wings,* 15.

There was no formal recruitment: Merryman, *Clipped Wings,* 14.

"it might be the straw": Merryman, *Clipped Wings,* 16.

"Many of them . . . squeezed in": Cole, *Women Pilots,* 13–14.

"How many hours of signed time" and all quotes until "Have you got a pen?": Cole, *Women Pilots,* 13.

One woman with bad vision: Cole, *Women Pilots,* 14.

8: WELCOME TO THE WASPS

When Gertrude arrived: Cole, *Women Pilots,* 3.

At Avenger Field Gertrude: Granger, *On Final Approach,* A-78/D.

As they entered the gates: Granger, *On Final Approach,* 96.

"Imagine an empty space": Cole, *Women Pilots,* 24

"Some thin young shoulders": Alberta Fitzgerald Head, "General Arnold Comes to Avenger Field," in *West Texas Historical Association Yearbook* (Lubbock, TX: West Texas Historical Association, 1994), 96–97.

Her face was burned dry: Granger, *On Final Approach,* 228.

Six women were assigned: Cole, *Women Pilots,* 24.

For early trainees, the program: Cole, *Women Pilots,* xiii.

For membership to flight training: "WASP Statistics," WASP on the Web, www.wingsacrossamerica.us/wasp/stats.htm; Granger, *On Final Approach,* A-100/N.

Weak Women?: Granger, *On Final Approach,* A102/P.

In 1944 Colonel Paul Tibbets: Cole, *Women Pilots,* 97.

There were some silly rules: Cole, *Women Pilots,* 32.

"We were all so anxious": Cole, *Women Pilots,* 32.

During the early flight classes: "Uniforms of the WASP of WWII," WASP on the Web, www.wingsacrossamerica.us/wasp/gallery/WASP%20Uniforms2.pdf.

Gertrude had little difficulty: Tompkins Whittall, interview by author, January 4, 2003.

She heard lectures: US Army Air Force document, *Uniform Code of Military Justice*, date missing.

"The plane won't kill you": Cole, *Women Pilots*, 36.

Despite her distance: Mickey Axton, interview by author, 2003.

Most of their instructors were male: Cole, *Women Pilots*, 26–27.

"They were black and blue": Cole, *Women Pilots*, 26–27.

"My first instructor drank too much": Cole, *Women Pilots*, 26–27

"Mr. J. R. Smith, an instructor": Cole, *Women Pilots*, 27.

"great big fleece-lined": Cole, *Women Pilots*, 36.

Some of the men: Cole, *Women Pilots*, 113–114.

Sabotage? Really: Cole, *Women Pilots*, 113–114.

"I don't think it was": Cole, *Women Pilots*, 45.

"The stories of sabotage": Cole, *Women Pilots*, 114.

The male officers made: Wood and Lewis, *We Were WASPs*, 17.

Meanwhile, Jacqueline Cochran: Granger, *On Final Approach*, 135.

9: BASIC AND ADVANCED TRAINING

"all of a sudden": Cole, *Women Pilots*, 40–41.

The BT washed out: Granger, *On Final Approach*, A-104/Q.

If Gertrude had mixed feelings: Mickey Axton, interview by author, 2003; Tony Holmes, *Jane's Historic Military Aircraft* (London: HarperCollins, 1998), 198.

"let go of what you feel": Mickey Axton, telephone interview by author, December 2002.

Some of the army air force men: Brinley and Cochran, *Jackie Cochran*, 210.

"None of us ever": Gertrude Tompkins, letter to Elizabeth Tompkins Whittall, undated but probably August or September, 1944.

"pulverized to jelly": Granger, *On Final Approach*, 108.

Each class sang its own distinctive song: Wood and Lewis, *We Were WASPs*, 24.

10: PECOS

Gertrude had applied: Tompkins Whittall, interview by author, 2002; Granger, *On Final Approach*, 281, A-55/B.

Gertrude was aware from her father's letters: Laura and Ken Whittall-Scherfee, interview by author, November 2002.

America's Industrial Might: Merryman, *Clipped Wings*, 8–11.

"If the wings stay on": Tompkins Whittall, interview by author, January 4, 2003.

The Paperback Book Goes to War: Yoni Applebaum, "Publishers Gave Away 122,951,031 Books During World War II," *Atlantic*, September 10, 2014, www.theatlantic.com/business/archive /2014/09/publishers-gave-away-122951031-books-during-world-war-ii/379893/.

11: ON SILVER WINGS

His name was Duncan Miller: Duncan Miller, interview by author, December 12, 2009; Laura and Ken Whittall-Scherfee, interviews by author, 2002 and 2003.

"ooh-la-la figure": Miller, interview by author, December 12, 2009.

"She had a great personality": Miller, interview by author, December 12, 2009.

"was considered a good pilot": Miller, interview by author, December 12, 2009.

Music and World War II: Manchester, *Glory and the Dream*, 376.

"Once you could do": Gertrude Tompkins, letter to Elizabeth Tompkins Whittall, undated but probably August or September, 1944.

Several hours later: Miller, interview by author, December 12, 2009.

There are tales: Axton, interview by author, 2003.

The year before, Henry's sister: Tompkins Whittall, interview by author, January 4, 2003; Laura Whittall-Scherfee, interview by author, November 2002; Ann Vreeland Wood, interview by author, July 2003.

Beauty Is a Duty: Caitlin L., "When Beauty Was a Duty: Cosmetic Appeal During WWII," XO Vain, December 2, 2014, www.xovain.com/makeup/womens-makeup-and-hairstyles-in-the-forties-world-war-two.

"carry the inherited burden": Tompkins Whittall, interview by author, January 4, 2003.

12: FLYING FOR HER COUNTRY

Mabel Rawlinson was a graduate: Granger, *On Final Approach*, A-105Q.

Ferrying Airplanes: Granger, *On Final Approach*, A-103/P.

"were ferrying the majority": Merryman, *Clipped Wings*, 23.

Some WASPs helped Russia: Granger, *On Final Approach*, 326.

WASP Hazel Ying Lee, flying a P-63: Granger, *On Final Approach*, 451.

Byrd Howell Granger, author of: Granger, *On Final Approach*, 326.

"Say, now, have you seen" and all quotes until *"Don't speak the same language":* Granger, *On Final Approach*, 326.

"All WASPs wondered": Noggle, *A Dance with Death: Soviet Airwomen in World War II*, loc. 23.

In Russia, women pilots: Noggle, *Dance with Death*, loc. 213–280.

Hundreds of letters of commendation: The WASP Program: An Historical Synopsis, Lt. Col. Dora Dougherty, cited in Merryman, *Clipped Wings*, 149.

General Hap Arnold wrote: Letter to each member of the WASPs, October 1, 1944, cited in Merryman, *Clipped Wings*, 115.

13. DILEMMA

From the beginning the WASPs: Quotes and material following are from Merryman, *Clipped Wings*, 31.

"I had expected militarization": Merryman, *Clipped Wings*, 33.

The women were trained: Army Air Force Central Flying Training Command, *History of the WASP Program*, (Washington, DC: 1945).

There was at least one proposal: Merryman, *Clipped Wings*, 39.

"loved to hate": Encyclopedia.com, "Cochran, Jacqueline," www.encyclopedia.com/women/encyclopedias-almanacs -transcripts-and-maps/cochran-jacqueline-c-1910-1980.

Both Nancy Harkness Love: Merryman, *Clipped Wings*, 31.

"as stenographers, telephone operators": Merryman, *Clipped Wings*, 36.

"insult society women": Merryman, *Clipped Wings*, 36.

"You are going to start": Merryman, *Clipped Wings*, 37.

"Are we to deny": Merryman, *Clipped Wings*, 37.

"taking the jobs": Granger, *On Final Approach*, 392.

"The government has spent": Granger, *On Final Approach*, 429.

"embarrassing to women pilots": Granger, *On Final Approach*, 149.

"represents a very curious": T.M.P., "Movie Review: At Loew's Criterion," *New York Times*, March 16, 1944, www.nytimes .com/movie/review?res=9903E4DA113CE03ABC4E52DFB56 6838F659EDE.

Gertrude sensed the growing desire: Ken and Laura Whittall-Scherfee, interview by author, 2002.

After sending his initial letter and material following: Tompkins Whittall, telephone interviews by author, 2003.

"The atmosphere was heavy": Whittall, *From There to Here*, 21.

"Obedience was the norm": Tompkins Whittall, interview by author, January 4, 2003.

"*She had made a promise*": Laura Whittall Scherfee, note to the author, 30 November 2015.

After her marriage and all quotes until "*Henry was very much pleased*": Gertrude Tompkins, letter to Elizabeth Tompkins Whittall, 20 October 1944, Whittall family collection.

14: SEIZED BY THE SUN

A month had passed: Teletype, Sixth Fighter Group, Long Beach, US Army Air Force, dated October 26, 1944.

The next day she would: US Army Air Force, Report of Major Accident, Form 14, dated October 26, 1944.

"*Tower, this is Mustang 669*": Missing Aircraft Report, US Army Air Force, date on document obscured.

The weather was good: Pat Macha, telephone interviews by author, 2003.

It was four days before: Gary Patric Macha and Don Jordan, *Aircraft Wrecks in the Mountains and Deserts of California, 1909–2002*, 3rd ed. (Lake Forest, CA: Info Net Publishing, 2002), 169. This later edition is dedicated to Gertrude Tompkins Silver.

There was confusion over the number: Brig. Gen. Bob E. Nowland, US Army Air Force, letter marked CONFIDENTIAL to Commanding General, Air Transport Command, 31 October 1944, author's collection.

15: SEARCHING

It was assumed that Gerturde: 31 Teletype Messages (TWX) on search, October 30, 1944–November 20, 1944.

On November 16: Teletype, Sixth Fighter Group Long Beach, US Army Air Force. November 17, 1944.

By November 18: US Army Air Force fatality report, November 30, 1944.

Henry wrote to the air force: Henry Silver, letter to US Air Force, 14 December 1944.

"Your letter to WASP Gertrude": US Air Force, letter to Duncan Miller, 12 December 1944.

"memory of those WASP" and all quotes until *"I hope you will always feel":* General H. H. Arnold, letter to Henry Silver, 12 January 1945.

Macha, a retired Huntington Beach: Pat Macha, interviews by author, 2002–2015.

Macha began building a database: Website for Macha's work: www.aircraftwrecks.com.

"We contacted him": Ken and Laura Whittall-Scherfee, interview by author, November, 2002.

"The 51 is a very hot plane": Macha, interviews by author, 2002–2015.

Meanwhile, Laura contacted: Laura Whittall-Scherfee, letter to Dana Rohrabacher, 9 July 1998; Dana Rohrabacher, letter to Laura Whittall-Scherfee, 28 July 1998; Rear Admiral Gene R. Kendall, letter to Dana Rohrabacher, 24 September 1998.

"It is metal, all right": Jim Blunt, interview by author, 2003.

In 1999 Gary Fabian: UB88 Project website, http://ub88.org.

Using MBS, in 2001: Gary Fabian, interviews by author, 2014–2015.

"This event left a very strong" and all quotes until *"It was definitely that year":* "Memory Assists in the Search for Lost Plane," February 27, 2005, *Daily Breeze* article posted on www.aircraftwrecks.com.

"We took a heading on it and began to search" and all quotes until *"We were crossing targets off our list":* Macha, interviews by author, 2002–2015.

"We've scoured the bay": Fabian, interviews by author, 2014–2015.

"It's fascinated all of us": Fabian, interviews by author, 2014–2015.

EPILOGUE

"Be sure and look for Gertrude!": Whittall, *From There to Here*, 20.

At a WASP reunion in 2002: Laura and Ken Whittall-Scherfee, Mickey Axton, Winifred Wood, Betty Tackaberry Blake, Lela Lowder Harding, interviews by author, 2003.

"I can't forget that there" and all quotes until *"Perhaps it was because she was older"*: Laura and Ken Whittall-Scherfee, Mickey Axton, Winifred Wood, Betty Tackaberry Blake, Lela Lowder Harding, interviews by author, 2003.

"We need to find Gertrude": Axton, interview by author, 2003.

AFTERWORD

"so many stories": Ann Vreeland Wood, interview by author, July 2003.

"It was an experience": Laura Whittall-Scherfee, interview by author, September 2015.

BIBLIOGRAPHY

BOOKS

Brinley, Maryann Bucknum, and Jacqueline Cochran. *Jackie Cochran: The Autobiography of the Greatest Woman Pilot in History*. New York, Bantam Books, 1987.

Cole, Jean Hascall. *Women Pilots of World War II*. Salt Lake City: University of Utah Press, 1992.

Davis, Larry, and Don Greer. *Walk Around: P-51D, Walk Around No. 7*. Carrollton, TX: Squadron/Signals, 1995.

Granger, Byrd Howell. *On Final Approach: The Women Air Force Service Pilots of World War II*. Scottsdale, AZ: Falconer, 1991.

Gilbert, Martin. *A History of the Twentieth Century*. Vol. 2. New York: Avon, 1998.

Kinzey, Bert. *P-51 Mustang*. Carrollton, TX: Squadron/Signal, 1996.

Landdeck, Katherine Sharp. "Experiment in the Cockpit: The Women Air Force Service Pilots of World War II." In *The Airplane in American Culture*, edited by Dominick Pisano, 165–98. Ann Arbor: University of Michigan Press, 2003.

Manchester, William. *The Glory and the Dream: A Narrative History of America, 1932–1972*. Vol. 1. Boston: Little, Brown, 1973.

Merryman, Mollie. *Clipped Wings: The Rise and Fall of the Women Airforce Service Pilots (WASPs) of World War II*. New York: New York University Press, 1998.

Noggle, Anne. *A Dance with Death: Soviet Airwomen in World War II*. College Station, TX: Texas A&M University Press, 2002. Kindle version.

Whittall, Elizabeth Tompkins. *From There to Here*. Smithtown, NY: Exposition Press, 1981.

Wood, M. Winifred, and Dorothy Swain Lewis. *We Were WASPs*. Printed by authors, 1978.

INTERVIEWS

Jim Blunt, telephone interview with author, 2003.

Dr. Judith Duchan, telephone interview with author, January 20, 2003.

Gary Fabian, telephone interviews with author, 2014–2015.

Pat Macha, telephone interviews with author, 2003–2015.

Duncan Miller, telephone interview with author, December 5, 2009.

Elizabeth Tompkins Whittall, telephone interviews with author, 2002–2005.

Laura Whittall-Scherfee and Ken Whittall Scherfee, telephone and personal interviews with author, 2002–2015.

DOCUMENTS

Driscoll, John J., Lieutenant, US Army Air Force, letter to Duncan Miller, 12 December 1944. National Archives, Veterans Service Records.

Geary, Terence, and Andy Hailey. *Report of Major Accident, October 26, 1944.* US Army Air Force. 2003. www.icc.net/`cahailey /WASP_KIA/GVTTompkins.html. Website discontinued. Printout in author's collection.

Kendall, Gene R., Rear Admiral, US Navy, letter to Congressman Dana Rohrabacher, 24 September 1998. Author's collection. Cites costs of search.

Kolendorski, Stanley Michael, letter to author containing Royal Air Force information about his uncle, 1 August 2003. Author's collection.

Rohrabacher, Dana, letter to G. Pat Macha on navy response, 22 October 1998. Author's collection.

Rohrabacher, Dana, letter to Laura Whittall-Scherfee regarding request for navy assistance in search for Gertrude Tompkins, 28 July 1998. Author's collection.

Tompkins Whittall, Elizabeth, and Paul Whittall, letter to Laura Whittall-Scherfee, 2 April 2010. Author's collection.

US Army Air Force. *Academic Training Record—WASP Training Course, Gertrude Tompkins, Class 43-W-7.* Date missing. Author's collection.

US Army Air Force. *Missing Aircraft Report.* Date on document obscured, but probably October 31, 1944.

US Army Air Force. *Pilot Operation Instructions, North American P-51 Mustang.* 1943.

US Army Air Force. 31 teletype messages (TWXs) on the search. Dated from 30 October 1944 to 20 November 1944. Author's collection.

Yount, Barton K., Commanding General, US Army Air Forces Training Command. Speech to last graduating class of WASPs. December 7, 1944.

NEWSPAPERS

New Zealand newspaper clipping. c. 1933. In possession of Elizabeth Tompkins Whittall's granddaughter, Laura Whittall-Scherfee. Newspaper's name is unknown.

Merl, Jean. "Aviation Buffs Hope to Discover Fate of Female War Pilot Who Vanished After Takeoff in 1944." *Los Angeles Times.* September 19, 2002.

WEBSITES AND OTHER RESOURCES

Bond, Jill. *We Served Too: The Story of the Women Airforce Pilots of World War II.* Documentary film. www.wstthemovie.com.

Bravo 369 Flight Foundation website. www.bravo369.org.

Duchan, Judith. "History of Speech-Pathology." State University of New York at Buffalo. May 12, 2011. www.acsu.buffalo.edu/~duchan/new_history/overview.html.

Fabian, Gary, multibeam sonar searches, http://ub88.org/. Photos of historic wrecks using US Geological Service data. Also www.bathymetricresearch.com and www.facebook.com/bathymetricresearch. The seafloor revealed with multibeam sonar.

"Kermie Cam—P 51C Mustang—Part 3." YouTube video. 11:45. Posted by "Kermit Weeks Videos." October 7, 2012. www.youtube.com/watch?v=eOXxUApaaWo&feature=youtube.

Landdeck, Katherine Sharp. Texas Women's University faculty page. November 7, 2016. www.twu.edu/research/katherine-sharp-landdeck.asp.

Macha, G. Pat. "Aircraft Wrecks in the Mountains and Deserts of the American West." www.aircraftwrecks.com. This site has numerous photos and videos of airplane wrecks in the Western states, as well as comprehensive information on each downed aircraft.

"Nancy Harkness Love." http://en.wikipedia.org/wiki/Nancy _Harkness_Love.

National Public Radio. "A Contraband Camera: Photos of World War II WASP." The Picture Show. March 10, 2010. www.npr .org/sections/pictureshow/2010/03/a_contraband_camera _photos_of.html.

National WASP World War II Museum website. http://wasp museum.org.

Official Archive, Women Airforce Service Pilots. Texas Women's University Libraries. www.twu.edu/library/wasp.asp.

"P-51 Mustangs in the air—The P-51 Mustang Video—'Sketches of Freedom.'" YouTube video. 4:05. Posted by "gregersgram." July 29, 2009. www.youtube.com/watch?v=xITLBRkOd2k.

"P-51 Pilot Reports." Warbird Alley. www.warbirdalley.com /articles/p51pr.htm.

Stamberg, Susan. "Female WWII Pilots: The Original Fly Girls." National Public Radio: Around the Nation and broadcast on *Morning Edition.* March 9, 2010. www.npr.org/2010/03/09 /123773525/female-wwii-pilots-the-original-fly-girls.

US Army Air Force, First Motion Picture Unit. *Flight Characteristics of the P-51 Airplane.* 1944. www.zenoswarbirdvideos.com/.

Wackerfuss, Dr. Andrew T. "Women's Airforce Service Pilots." Air Force Historical Support Division Fact Sheet. September 8, 2015. www.afhso.af.mil/topics/factsheets/factsheet .asp?id=15244.

WASP on the Web. www.wingsacrossamerica.us/wasp/index
.htm.
"Women Air Force Service Pilots." https://en.wikipedia.org
/wiki/Women_Airforce_Service_Pilots.

ADDITIONAL READING

*A WASP Among Eagles: A Woman Military Test Pilot in World War
II*, by WASP Ann Baumgartner Carl.

Dear Mother and Daddy, by WASP Marie Clark.

Flying High, by Betty Greene with Dietrich Buss.

Flying the Zuni Mountains, by Ann Darr.

*For God, Country and the Thrill of It: Women Airforce Service Pilots
in World War II*, Photo portraits and text by WASP Anne
Noggle.

Girls Can't Be Pilots: An Aeriobiography, by WASP Margaret J.
Ringenberger with Jane L. Roth.

Girls of Avenger, by WASP Alyce Roher.

*How High She Flies: Dorothy Swain Lewis, WASP of World War II,
Horsewoman, Artist, Teacher*, by Ann L. Cooper with Dorothy
Swain Lewis.

*Love at First Flight: One Woman's Experience as a WASP in World
War II and Fifty Years Later She's Still Flying*, by WASP Elizabeth Strohfus as told to Cheryl Young.

Out of the Blue and Into History, by WASP Betty Stagg Turner.

Sisters of the Sky, Volumes I and II, by WASP Adela Rick Scharr.

WASP Letters Home, by WASP Bee Haydu.

*WASPs in Their Own Words: An Illustrated History of the Women
Airforce Service Pilots of WWII*, by Nancy Parrish.

WASPS: Women Airforce Service Pilots in World War II, by Vera S.
Williams.

Wings, WASPs and Warriors, by Travis Moody.

Wingtip to Wingtip: 8 WASPs, Women's Airforce Service Pilots of World War II, by Marjorie H. Roberts.

Winning My Wings: A Woman Airforce Service Pilot in World War II, by WASP Marion Stegemen Hodgson.

Women Airforce Service Pilots of World War II, the WASP, by J. David Dameron.

Women Aviators: 26 Stories of Pioneer Flights, Daring Missions, and Record-Setting Journeys, by Karen Bush Gibson.

Women Who Dared: American Female Test Pilots, Flight Test Engineers, and Astronauts, by Lt. Col. Yvonne "Pat" Pateman, USAF (retired).

Yankee Doodle Gals: Women Pilots of World War II, by Amy Nathan.

Zoot-Suits and Parachutes and Wings of Silver, Too! The World War II Air Force Training of Women Pilots, 1942–1944, by WASP Doris Brinker Tanner.

INDEX